Funded by a State Legislature Grant
Senator Suzi Oppenheimer

RYE FREE READING ROOM
*Escape to the Library*

*Bloom's*

# GUIDES

Sylvia Plath's
# The Bell Jar

The Adventures of
    Huckleberry Finn
All the Pretty Horses
Animal Farm
The Autobiography of Malcolm X
The Awakening
The Bell Jar
Beloved
Beowulf
Brave New World
The Canterbury Tales
Catch-22
The Catcher in the Rye
The Chosen
The Crucible
Cry, the Beloved Country
Death of a Salesman
Fahrenheit 451
Frankenstein
The Glass Menagerie
The Grapes of Wrath
Great Expectations
The Great Gatsby
Hamlet
The Handmaid's Tale
Heart of Darkness
The House on Mango Street
I Know Why the Caged Bird Sings
The Iliad
Invisible Man
Jane Eyre

The Kite Runner
Lord of the Flies
Macbeth
Maggie: A Girl of the Streets
The Member of the Wedding
The Metamorphosis
Native Son
Night
1984
The Odyssey
Oedipus Rex
Of Mice and Men
One Hundred Years of Solitude
Pride and Prejudice
Ragtime
A Raisin in the Sun
The Red Badge of Courage
Romeo and Juliet
The Scarlet Letter
A Separate Peace
Slaughterhouse-Five
Snow Falling on Cedars
The Stranger
A Streetcar Named Desire
The Sun Also Rises
A Tale of Two Cities
The Things They Carried
To Kill a Mockingbird
Uncle Tom's Cabin
The Waste Land
Wuthering Heights

*Bloom's*
# GUIDES

## Sylvia Plath's
# The Bell Jar

Edited & with an Introduction
by Harold Bloom

BLOOM'S
LITERARY CRITICISM
*An imprint of Infobase Publishing*

**Bloom's Guides: The Bell Jar**

Copyright © 2009 by Infobase Publishing

Introduction © 2009 by Harold Bloom

All rights reserved. No part of this book may be reproduced or utilized in any form or by any means, electronic or mechanical, including photocopying, recording, or by any information storage or retrieval systems, without permission in writing from the publisher. For information contact:

Bloom's Literary Criticism
An imprint of Infobase Publishing
132 West 31st Street
New York, NY 10001

**Library of Congress Cataloging-in-Publication Data**
Sylvia Plath's The bell jar / edited and with an introduction
by Harold Bloom.
    p. cm. — (Bloom's guides)
  Includes bibliographical references and index.
  ISBN 978-1-60413-203-8
  1. Plath, Sylvia. Bell jar. I. Bloom, Harold.
  PS3566.L27B438 2009
  813'.54—dc22

                              2008036547

Bloom's Literary Criticism books are available at special discounts when purchased in bulk quantities for businesses, associations, institutions, or sales promotions. Please call our Special Sales Department in New York at (212) 967-8800 or (800) 322-8755.

You can find Bloom's Literary Criticism on the World Wide Web at
http://www.chelseahouse.com

Contributing Editor: Amy Sickels
Cover design by Takeshi Takahashi
Printed in the United States of America
Bang EJB 10 9 8 7 6 5 4 3 2 1
This book is printed on acid-free paper.

All links and Web addresses were checked and verified to be correct at the time of publication. Because of the dynamic nature of the Web, some addresses and links may have changed since publication and may no longer be valid.

# Contents

Introduction                                                          7

Biographical Sketch                                                   9

The Story Behind the Story                                           12

List of Characters                                                   15

Summary and Analysis                                                 18

Critical Views                                                       59

   Howard Moss on Illness and Disclosure in the Novel     59

   Vance Bourjaily on Pseudonyms and
     Alternate Identities                     63

   Robert Scholes on Plath's Use of Realism             66

   Linda W. Wagner on the Female Coming-of-Age
     Novel                                    69

   E. Miller Budick on Plath's Feminist Discourse       80

   Diane S. Bonds on Esther's Tentative Rebirth         92

   Paula Bennett on Models of Womanhood                103

   Pat Macpherson on the Portrayal of Social and
     Gender Conventions                      112

   Tim Kendall on Esther's Search for Identity         121

   Marilyn Boyer on Language and Disability            128

   Kate A. Baldwin on the Novel's Social and
     Political Contexts                      140

   Janet Badia on Pop Culture Appropriations of
     *The Bell Jar*                           151

Works by Sylvia Plath                                               161

Annotated Bibliography                                              162

Contributors                                                        165

Acknowledgments                                                     168

Index                                                               170

# Introduction

HAROLD BLOOM

I attempted to read *The Bell Jar* in 1971 when it was published, in the United States, some eight years after Sylvia Plath's suicide. Though I recall being unable to get very far with it then, one learns to be more dispassionate as old age augments, and I have just completed reading Plath's novel, thirty-seven years farther on in life. I see why it is popular with so many who identify themselves with the protagonist, who plainly is Plath a decade before her death.

*The Bell Jar* is a period piece, a portrait of the poet as a very young woman in the long-vanished United States of the 1950s. Though Plath is regarded by many as a permanent poet, I myself am not of that persuasion. It seems to me not possible to discover any aesthetic merit in *The Bell Jar*. Since the book is so popular, for now, its historical, sociological, clinical, and ideological interest can be acknowleged.

It is always a little painful, for me, to place a worthy but inadequate book in an authentically critical perspective. Of the critical views excerpted in this Guide, I think best of Howard Moss's comments, if only because he has read the book I have just tried to absorb and sees "that Esther is cut off from the instinct for sympathy right from the beginning—for herself as well as for others." I also note that Moss registers the obsessive imagery of babies throughout the book. Those images clash with the emotion of disgust that Moss astutely characterizes: "disgust that has not yet become contempt and is therefore more damaging."

I would add that the damage is also aesthetic, since only a realist as powerful and ultimately phantasmagoric as a Zola or a Dreiser can transmute a fictive character's emotion of disgust into an affect that can sustain universal interest, which is a requisite for the novel as an art. Admirers of *The Bell Jar* have compared it to Charlotte Brontë's *Jane Eyre*, a juxtaposition that obliterates Plath's book. The effect is rather like equally injurious efforts to compare Plath's verse to poets of the eminence of Wallace Stevens, Elizabeth Bishop, and May Swenson.

# Biographical Sketch

Sylvia Plath was born on October 27, 1932, in Jamaica Plain, Massachusetts, to Aurelia Schober Plath, a first-generation American of Austrian descent, and Otto Emile Plath, an immigrant from Grabow, Germany. Plath's brother, Warren, was born two and a half years later. Plath's father was a professor of zoology and German at Boston University and a noted bee specialist, and her mother was an avid reader. In 1936, during the Great Depression, the family moved to Winthrop, Massachusetts, where Plath spent most of her childhood. She was raised a Unitarian Christian. At the age of eight, Plath published her first poem in the Sunday *Boston Herald*'s children's section.

Her father, characterized by Plath as authoritarian, died of diabetes in 1940, a week and a half after Plath's eighth birthday. Her mother was offered a job to teach in the medical-secretarial training program at Boston University, and the family moved to Wellesley, Massachusetts. In high school, Plath wrote poetry and short stories. She was a model student, winning prizes and scholarships, and attended Smith College on a scholarship from 1950–1955. In 1953, she spent a summer as guest editor at *Mademoiselle* magazine in New York City, after winning a short story contest. Many of the events that took place that summer were the inspiration for *The Bell Jar*. After returning home from New York, Plath fell into a deep depression when she learned she was not accepted into Frank O'Connor's summer writing class at Harvard University. She then suffered a mental breakdown, which led to her first medically documented suicide attempt. She was briefly committed to a facility where she received electroconvulsive therapy. Plath returned to school and graduated from Smith in 1955, with honors, and won a Fulbright scholarship to Newnham College in Cambridge, England.

While pursuing graduate studies, she met the English poet Ted Hughes, and they were married on June 16, 1956. In the early years of her marriage, Plath started writing poetry more seriously. She and Hughes moved to the United States, where Plath taught at Smith College for a while, and then the couple moved to Boston, where Plath audited poetry classes taught by Robert Lowell. Plath and Hughes returned to England when they found out that Plath was pregnant, and she gave birth to her daughter, Frieda Rebecca, in April 1960. Plath also published her first collection of poems, *The Colossus*, in 1960. In 1961, Plath suffered a miscarriage. Around the same time, Alfred Knopf bought the rights to publish *The Colossus* in the United States, and Plath started working intensely on *The Bell Jar*. She gave birth to her son, Nicholas Farrar, in 1962.

Plath's marriage to Hughes was rife with difficulty, and she felt distressed by his admission of infidelity. They separated in 1962, and Plath moved to an apartment in London with the two children. In 1963, *The Bell Jar* was published under the pseudonym Victoria Lucas in England. Disillusioned by her failed marriage, burdened financially, and struggling to care for her children, Plath committed suicide on February 11, 1963, by ingesting sleeping pills and placing her head in the oven while the gas was turned on. She was thirty years old.

After her death, Hughes, still legally her husband, became the executor of Plath's estate, a development that proved at times to be controversial. A year after her death, her well-known poems "Lady Lazarus" and "Daddy" appeared. *Ariel* was published in 1965, Hughes making the decision about which poems to include and how to order them. The book became a classic work of modern American poetry, loosely connecting Plath to the confessional poets, including Robert Lowell, Anne Sexton, and John Berryman. This publication was followed by *Three Women: A Monologue of Three Voices* (1968), *Crossing the Water* (1971), and *Winter Trees* (1971). Hughes also convinced Plath's mother to publish *The Bell Jar* in the United States, where it appeared in 1971 and has sold more than 2 million copies.

Aurelia collected and edited her daughter's correspondence and published them as *Letters Home* in 1975. *The Collected Poems* was published in 1981, and a year later Plath became the first poet to win a Pulitzer Prize posthumously. In 1982, Hughes edited *The Journals of Sylvia Plath*, withholding portions of her journals from the public until a month before he died in 1998. Karen V. Kukil then edited and published *The Unabridged Journals of Sylvia Plath* in 2000.

In the last seven years of her life, Sylvia Plath wrote more than 250 poems, nonfiction pieces, short stories, and a novel. She also wrote extensively in her journals and produced an abundance of letters, mostly to her mother. Although Plath only published one book of poetry during her life, her posthumously published poems and *The Bell Jar* have made her one of America's most critically acclaimed writers. Sylvia Plath's gravestone is in Yorkshire, England, with Ted Hughes's name chipped off, the vandalism most likely carried out by one or several of her enduring fans.

The Story Behind the Story

*The Bell Jar* was first published in the United States, almost ten years after Sylvia Plath's death, exploding on the bestseller charts. Today its popularity endures, and the novel has sold more than 2 million copies in the United States alone. Plath started writing the highly autobiographical novel after her first book of poetry, *The Colossus*, was published in 1960. *The Bell Jar* was first published in England under the pseudonym Victoria Lucas in 1963. Plath used the pen name to protect people portrayed in the book and possibly also because she doubted its literary merit, referring to it in a letter as "a pot boiler." One month after its publication, Plath committed suicide.

*The Bell Jar* is often considered a roman à clef, with Esther Greenwood's descent into mental illness paralleling Plath's own experiences. The events in the novel closely parallel Plath's twentieth year, and the novel contains many descriptions of real people, though Plath changed names and embellished fictional details. For example, like Esther who secures a high-profile summer internship at the magazine *Ladies' Day*, Plath worked in 1953 on the college editorial board at *Mademoiselle*. Philomena Guinea is based on Plath's patron, Olive Higgins Prouty, author of *Stella Dallas* and *Now, Voyager*, who funded Plath's scholarship to study at Smith College. Also similar to the novel's protagonist, Plath was rejected from a Harvard writing course taught by Frank O'Connor, which contributed greatly to her impending breakdown. Doctor Nolan is thought to be based on Plath's own therapist, Ruth Beuscher, whom she continued seeing into adulthood. Esther Greenwood's breakdown and suicide attempt closely resemble Plath's during the summer of her junior year. Plath swallowed an excessive dose of pills and hid in the crawlspace of the cellar, her absence prompting an all-out search by family, friends, and local officials. Two days later, she was discovered—alive, but semicomatose—and rushed to the hospital.

*The Bell Jar* has a noteworthy publishing history. In London, under the name of Victoria Lucas, it received moderately positive reviews and sold briefly. It was then published again in England, posthumously, in 1967, this time under Plath's name. In 1971, Ted Hughes, Plath's husband, convinced her mother, Aurelia, to allow *The Bell Jar* to be published in the United States. Aurelia worried that the novel's often unkind portraits of people would be injurious both to those portrayed and to Plath's growing reputation as a serious poet. Between the novel's publication in England and the United States, Plath's posthumous volume of poems, *Ariel*, had been published in 1965 to critical success. Reviewers praised the chilling, intimate, confessional poems, and many considered Plath to be a gifted writer. Though her poetry was by then being read and discussed in literary circles, *The Bell Jar* was almost unheard of in the United States until its publication in 1971. Its appearance would quickly make Plath a popular and tragic legend, to be adored by fans and debated by critics.

*The Bell Jar*'s reception in the United States was greatly affected by both the publicity surrounding Plath's death and the posthumous publication of *Ariel*. Bantam Books brought out an initial paperback edition in April 1972, with a print run of 357,000 copies. That initial printing sold out, as did a second and a third printing, in one month, and the novel remained on the bestseller list for at least 24 weeks.

Plath's suicide helped fuel her legendary status. The emotional immediacy of her confessional poems and the biography of the all-American girl who killed herself at the age of 30 add up to a tragic and compelling story. Plath has become a mythical cultlike figure: an artist who struggled through depression, overcame it, and was then destroyed by it. *The Bell Jar* is widely read among adolescent women. Esther Greenwood is a popular protagonist, the female counterpart to J.D. Salinger's Holden Caulfield. Esther is a good student, funny, sexually confused, and depressed. She often feels alienated from and pressured by society, and many young readers feel they can identify with her. The nervous breakdown and attempted suicide of a well-behaved, bright, and successful college student touches adolescent readers, and reading Sylvia Plath has become a rite of passage for many young adults.

Even for critics and scholars, the biography of Plath and her mythical stature greatly influence their readings of the novel. Critics have debated if the novel should be considered serious literature or if it should be remembered as a popular novel by an author whose true talent was poetry. *The Bell Jar* has received less scholarly attention than the poems, yet many notable critics have claimed it to be an important American novel that gives voice to women who are typically silenced. Feminist critics have analyzed the novel as a powerful critique of the repression of women in the 1950s and as a portrayal of one woman's struggle within such a society and her attempt to assert control over her life. Plath's highly respected poems, her tragic suicide a month after *The Bell Jar*'s initial publication, and the widely known story of her depression, breakdown, and stay in a mental hospital are impossible for readers to ignore in their reading of the book. As Sylvia Plath's only novel, *The Bell Jar* has become iconic in both literary and popular culture.

# List of Characters

**Esther Greenwood** is the protagonist and narrator of the novel. She has just finished her junior year in college and is spending a month in New York City to work at a fashion magazine. Smart, witty, astute, and socially insecure, Esther dreams of becoming a poet and traveling the world, but pressures to conform to the 1950s ideals of what a woman should be complicate this pursuit. Uncertainty, depression, and a growing sense of unreality plague Esther as she struggles with questions of identity and womanhood. The novel chronicles Esther's descent into mental illness and her struggle to overcome it. It is also a coming-of-age story, depicting Esther's disastrous encounters with men as she questions marriage, motherhood, and sex. In the end, she is tentatively released from her despair and reaches a more confident understanding of her self and her place in the world.

**Mrs. Greenwood** is Esther's mother. Since her husband's death, she has taught typing and shorthand in order to pay the bills. Mrs. Greenwood is practical and traditional. She loves her daughter but does not understand her. She would like to pretend that Esther's stay in the mental hospital never happened.

**Buddy Willard**, Esther's college boyfriend, attends Yale medical school. Athletic and conventional, Buddy believes a wife's sole duty is to support her husband. After contracting tuberculosis, Buddy spends time in a sanitarium. When Esther visits him, he proposes marriage, but Esther believes he is a hypocrite because he was deceitful about his previous sexual experiences.

**Mrs. Willard**, Buddy's mother, is a tweed-wearing, matronly woman, who dispenses maxims about how women must support their husbands. She represents the traditional wife and mother, and Esther views her as a floor mat that gets trampled by men.

**Doreen**, Esther's friend at the magazine in New York, is a blond, beautiful, southern college student who tries to help Esther in her relations with men. Esther and Doreen share a cynical outlook. Doreen rebels against societal convention, an attitude that Esther admires but does not entirely embrace.

**Betsy**, from Kansas, also works at the magazine with Esther. She is sweet and wholesome, Doreen's opposite. She is Esther's "innocent" friend. Esther in some ways relates to her more than she does Doreen but cannot understand Betsy's optimism.

**Jay Cee**, Esther's boss and editor of *Ladies' Day* magazine, wants Esther to be more ambitious. She represents the typical career woman: ambitious, confident, and professional. She treats Esther brusquely but kindly.

**Constantin**, a United Nations simultaneous interpreter, takes Esther out for dinner. He is thoughtful, kind, and accomplished but seems to be sexually uninterested in her.

**Marco**, a tall, handsome Peruvian, takes Esther on a date to a country club. Violent and sadistic, Marco is a misogynist. He tries to rape Esther, but she fights him off.

**Doctor Gordon**, Esther's first psychiatrist, is handsome and conceited and seems uninterested in Esther's symptoms. He barely speaks to her and bungles the electroshock therapy session. Doctor Gordon represents the patriarchal power of the medical establishment. After the shock treatment, Esther refuses to see him again.

**Philomena Guinea**, Esther's patron, is a famous, wealthy, elderly novelist. She funds Esther's scholarship and pays for Esther to go to a private hospital instead of the state institution.

**Doctor Nolan**, Esther's psychiatrist at the private hospital, is kind, sympathetic, and helpful. A progressive woman, she gives Esther the support and understanding she needs. Esther sees her as a mother figure and grows to trust and love Doctor Nolan.

**Joan Gilling**, a large, athletic, "horsy" woman, once dated Buddy Willard and becomes a patient at the private hospital with Esther. Esther feels both repulsed by and drawn to her. Joan emerges as Esther's double. After Joan's suicide, Esther must face the reality of death and her own desire to live.

**Irwin**, tall and not particularly caring, is a mathematics professor with whom Esther chooses to have physical relations because he seems intelligent and experienced and because he is a stranger. When she tells him she does not want to see him again, she feels more free and confident.

# Summary and Analysis

## 1

Sylvia Plath's *The Bell Jar* is an autobiographical novel that portrays six months in the life of nineteen-year-old Esther Greenwood, chronicling her breakdown, suicide attempts, and hospitalization. It takes place in New York City and the suburbs of Boston at the height of the cold war. A bildungsroman, or coming-of-age novel, *The Bell Jar* is recognized for its depiction of teenage angst, its exploration of the restricted role of women in 1950s society, and its unflinching portrayal of mental illness and the medical establishment. Esther, pressured by society and family to conform to their expectations, experiences a psychological rift and a crisis of identity.

The novel opens during the summer of 1953, the year that Julius and Ethel Rosenberg were executed. Esther, working at *Ladies' Day*, a fashion magazine in New York, finds it impossible to be one of the typical college girls of the 1950s whose education is stopped by marriage and motherhood, yet she feels too uncertain to strike out on a different path. From a feminist perspective, the novel is a critique of marriage, motherhood, and the patriarchal medical establishment. Esther feels pushed toward assuming different stereotypical female roles, each one exclusive from the other, which leads to a sense of fragmented identity and a destabilized state of mind. Unable to fit into the glittery world of New York or the stifling suburbs of Massachusetts, she eventually plunges into depression and experiences a breakdown.

*The Bell Jar* focuses on both the social and psychological, portraying American womanhood in the 1950s and documenting Esther's struggle to assert her own identity in a world that limits her choices because of her sex. Critic Janet Badia argues:

> From her relationship with Buddy Willard and her mother, to her experimentation with suicide methods, to her fight to escape the bell jar, nearly all the plot

episodes within the novel reveal Esther's struggles to gain control over her own life, to determine her own choices, rather than merely to accept those that society presents to her. In fact, one could argue that it is Esther's desire and search for control that threads together the many identities Esther struggles with, including her identity as a young woman, a patient, a daughter, a successful student, an aspiring writer, and, of course, a potential wife and mother. (132)

Critic Paula Bennett also attests that "the novel's principal focus is on the heroine's interaction with the world at large and particularly on the pressure put on young women in our culture to conform to a stereotyped view of femininity if they wish to achieve social, as opposed to professional, success" (124). Plath's novel raises questions about identity, sex, and mental illness, while presenting this period of confusion, disintegration, and renewal in Esther Greenwood's life.

*The Bell Jar*, consisting of 20 chapters, begins in the midst of Esther's month in New York. The first nine chapters record her time in the city, interspersed with flashbacks concerning her relationship with Buddy Willard and details of her academic achievements. This first half is more of a traditional coming-of-age story, but the structure is not a simple linear narrative. Parts of the novel move backward in time, revealing scenes from the past that have contributed to Esther's current weakened state of mind. These multiple layers of narrative present a mixture of external events and the internal workings of her mind in order to give life to two major themes in the novel: patriarchal society's pressures on women to conform to an oppressive role and the fragmentation of identity. The second half of the novel chronicles Esther's suicide attempts and her hospitalization, painting a picture of mental illness and its history of treatment in the 1950s.

The novel is told from the first-person perspective, allowing Esther to describe her mental breakdown firsthand. Esther's voice, detached, observant, and witty, reveals her complexity and intelligence, and her mental illness becomes real, even understandable, to the reader. Esther describes everything in the same matter-of-fact tone, whether describing a meal or documenting her suicide attempt. Critic Howard Moss explains, "Because it is written from the distraught observer's point of view rather than from the viewpoint of someone observing her, there is continuity to her madness; it is not one state suddenly supplanting another but the most gradual of processes" (179). The reader witnesses and follows the progression of her depressed state and withdrawal from reality, until she plunges into psychotic despair. While on the one hand, Esther is a reliable and trustworthy narrator, her conflicting actions also reveal her to be a master of deception. Esther feels she must perform in order to survive, but this constant acting eventually leads to her breakdown.

## 2

The novel begins in the summer of 1953, with Esther Greenwood, a junior at Smith College, living in New York City for a month. After winning a writing contest, she is a guest editor at *Ladies' Day* fashion magazine. Plath's first paragraph immediately establishes the potential conflict, the political and physical landscape, and the voice of Esther Greenwood: "It was a queer, sultry summer, the summer they electrocuted the Rosenbergs, and I didn't know what I was doing in New York. . . . I couldn't help wondering what it would be like, being burned alive all along your nerves. I thought it must be the worst thing in the world."

The novel takes place during the height of the cold war, adding an external element of tension and realism to the narrative. The Rosenbergs were convicted of spying for the Soviet Union and sentenced to death. The opening passage not only establishes the tense mood of the country but reveals Esther's worry and her preoccupation with death. Her fear of electrocution as "the worst thing in the world" resonates later when she undergoes electroshock therapy. As the narrative quickly reveals, although she is deeply upset by the execution, her mention of the Rosenbergs "is not merely a response to the electrocution of the Rosenbergs but to her own growing sense of alienation from the cultural demands and images of women with which she is daily bombarded during her guest editorship at *Ladies' Day*" (Bonds 51).

Esther and the eleven other contest winners are staying at what Esther calls the Amazon, a women's residence, with all expenses paid and an assortment of fashionable clothes and personal items. A studious, accomplished, all-American girl, Esther arrives in New York with high expectations. However, she quickly grows disappointed and estranged. She does not enjoy her new job or clothes and fears that "something was wrong with me." Esther, socially insecure and lacking self-confidence, feels displaced, and yet she understands that in society's eyes "I was supposed to be having the time of my life." These expectations and pressures conflict with her actual experiences: "I was supposed to be the envy of thousands of other college girls just like me all over America." She imagines that others would consider her lucky: "A girl lives in some out-of-the-way town for nineteen years, so poor she can't afford a magazine, and then she gets a scholarship to college and wins a prize here and a prize there and ends up steering New York like her own private car. Only I wasn't steering anything, not even myself." Instead of serving as a springboard for her career, Esther's time in New York edges her toward self-destruction and mental illness: "the disappointment of her New York experience is cataclysmic. Rather than shape her life, it nearly ends it; and Plath structures the novel to show the process of disenchantment in rapid acceleration" (Wagner 56).

Chapters 1 and 2 set up the juxtaposition between the ideal life that a talented, lucky American girl was "supposed" to expect and Esther's actual experiences. Instead of feeling dazzled by the freedom and glamour, Esther is obsessed with the death of the Rosenbergs, while the clothes she bought for her high-profile internship hang "limp as fish in my closet." New York should be a whirlwind of fun for a young woman, but Esther feels numb. Though she is able to pass in front of her friends as "normal" and happy enough, "I felt very still and very empty, the way the eye of a tornado must feel, moving dully along in the middle of the surrounding hullabaloo."

Esther frequently interrupts her New York story with interjections about Yale medical student Buddy Willard, her ex-boyfriend, though she has not officially broken up with him yet. Information about Buddy's significance to Esther's state of mind is revealed over the first nine chapters, but early on, Esther stirs the readers' curiosity when she claims that Buddy is responsible for her seeing "a cadaver's head," further establishing images of death and symbols of fragmentation.

In Chapter 1, Esther reveals that she is telling this story from a distant perspective. She refers to the many gifts from *Ladies' Day* that she hid away but "later, when I was all right again, I brought them out," reassuring the reader that she will survive her impending breakdown. Furthermore, the narrator mentions in an aside that she is now a mother: "last week I cut the plastic starfish off the sunglasses case for the baby to play with." Although the readers never hear anything more about this baby or her current life, this line confirms that she is at least a few years removed from the experiences she is describing.

Esther is a tall, attractive young woman, "skinny as a boy and barely rippled," and highly observant: "I liked looking on at other people in crucial situations. . . . I'd stop and look so hard I never forgot it." Though extremely smart and determined, she is also naïve and inexperienced. Esther feels out of place among the other, often privileged women at the hotel who are studying to work as secretaries, one of the few realistic options for a "working girl" in the 1950s. She describes one woman who was bored "with yachts and bored with flying around in airplanes" and admits, "I'm so jealous I can't speak." She is not only jealous of the woman's wealth but of her confidence and defined identity as well.

Chapter 1 establishes two important characters at the magazine: sassy southerner Doreen, who shares Esther's cynicism, and wholesome midwestern "good girl" Betsy, Doreen's opposite. The two women respectively symbolize a "type" of woman, and Esther absorbs, assumes, and mimics their polar-opposite identities, vacillating between the two and trying to act each part. Sharp-witted, beautiful Doreen is more mature and experienced with men and does not follow the rules a young woman of her time was expected to follow. Doreen's rebelliousness attracts Esther, but she cannot silence the thought that she is probably more like Betsy, "straight from Kansas with her bouncing blond ponytail and Sweetheart-of-Sigma-Chi smile."

Betsy continuously extends her friendship to Esther, but in Chapter 1, Esther prefers Doreen's cynicism: "She made me feel I was that much sharper than the others, and she really was wonderfully funny." Doreen and Esther skip out on the *Ladies' Day* party and instead go for a drink at a bar with Lenny Shepherd, a deejay who approaches their cab and is immediately attracted to Doreen. His friend, Frankie, expresses an interest in Esther, but she thinks he is too short and treats him coldly: "he was the type of fellow I can't stand." An example of Esther's inexperience and naiveté is made evident at the bar: She does not know anything about alcohol and is insecure about ordering a drink. She chooses straight vodka because she saw a picture of it in an advertisement, in which the vodka "looked clear and pure as water." Her yearning for what she thinks of as purity—to have a clean slate—is a recurring theme in the novel.

After a round of drinks, Esther accompanies Doreen and Lenny back to Lenny's apartment. Trying on a new identity, Esther calls herself Elly Higginbottom. Though Esther wants to be like Doreen, critic Linda W. Wagner suggests that the somewhat asexual name shows "instinctively that she wants to be protected from the kind of knowledge Doreen has" (57). Esther tries to be like Doreen but cannot convincingly enact the transformation: "Esther, sick unto death of her good girl image but unwilling or unable to shed it, flounders" (Bennett 124).

Chapter 2 takes place at Lenny's apartment "built exactly like the inside of a ranch." The strange setting contributes to Esther's feelings of disconnection: "Great white bearskins lay about underfoot, and the only furniture was a lot of low beds covered with Indian rugs." Stuffed animal heads instead of artwork are mounted on the walls, and, as Marilyn Boyer points out, "This trophy-mentality can be extended to the way in which Lenny treats Doreen. She too is a sort of prize" (202). Lenny, so self-centered that he puts on a tape of his own radio show, proceeds to jitterbug with Doreen, prompting her fiery independence to seemingly disappear. She is a passive object in his arms, and as she and Lenny dance, they "bang into each other and kiss and then swing to take a long drink." Esther, the outsider, watches until she drifts off to sleep. When she opens her eyes, the dance has spiraled into an animalistic scene of fighting and biting, and Doreen's breasts have slipped out of her dress. Esther feels repulsed: "She has psychologically disappeared at the experience of watching human beings be reduced to animals through violent, devolved, tribal behavior" (Boyer 202). Frightened and drunk, Esther leaves the apartment, determinedly walking the 46 blocks back to the Amazon.

In the elevator, Esther looks in the mirror to see "a big, smudgy-eyed Chinese woman staring idiotically into my face. It was only me, of course. I was appalled to see how wrinkled and used up I looked." Throughout the novel, the disembodied faces and distorted reflections in which she does not recognize herself are symbols of her struggle with an uncertain identity, "faces always associated with the threat of the loss of self" (Bonds 50). If she is having difficulty recognizing herself, she is also troubled by her lack of voice: "The silence depressed me. It wasn't the silence of silence. It was my own silence."

Back in her hotel room, Esther takes a bath and soon feels restored. The bath, symbolizing baptism, serves as a way to separate herself from the fallen Doreen and as a way to remember her true self: "I never feel so much myself as when I'm in a hot bath." She believes that she is "growing pure again," comparing the bath water to "holy water." After witnessing the drunken, animalistic interlude at Lenny's, she cleanses herself, noting, "I felt pure and sweet as a new baby." To be born again, she must dissociate from reality: "Doreen is dissolving, Lenny Shepherd is dissolving, Frankie is dissolving, New York is dissolving, they are all dissolving away and none of them matter any more."

After this symbolic baptism, Esther falls asleep and is awakened by a drunken Doreen pounding on her door and forcing Esther to return to the real world. Instead of bringing Doreen inside, "I decided the only thing to do was to dump her on the carpet." Esther continues, "I made a decision about Doreen that night. I decided I would watch her and listen to what she said, but deep down I would have nothing at all to do with her. Deep down, I would be loyal to Betsy and her innocent friends. It was Betsy I resembled at heart." Betsy, as a future homemaker and wife, represents the kind of young woman Esther feels pressured to be, one who will be rewarded for conformity. From this point, Esther attempts to extricate her identity from that of the unwholesome Doreen. The revulsion that Esther felt at Lenny's is symbolized in Doreen's vomit. The next morning, Doreen is gone, the carpet is clean "except for a faint, irregular dark stain before my door." The stain becomes symbolic of Esther's guilt: "The stain is indelible as is the fact that Esther, in the process of abandoning Doreen, has stigmatized her as undesirable" (Boyer 203–204). At this stage of the narrative, Esther's worry and unhappiness, her dissatisfaction with life, do not seem entirely unreasonable or unusual for a young woman to experience, and yet her feelings as an alienated observer and her dominating numbness also hint of more serious, potentially ominous forces at work.

## 3

Chapter 3 begins with the lavish *Ladies' Day* banquet luncheon: "Arrayed on the *Ladies' Day* banquet table were yellow-green avocado pear halves stuffed with crabmeat and mayonnaise and platters of rare roast beef and cold chicken, and every so often a cut-glass bowl heaped with black caviar." In the offices of a magazine primarily targeting homemakers, the staff gives the young women hints about cooking and cleaning, in expectation that they, too, will become housewives someday. The magazine staff has shown the girls "endless glossy kitchens" and "how difficult it is to photograph apple pie à la mode under bright lights," revealing the artifice behind the world of perfection and culinary accomplishment they are trying to present. Yet, food is a way to fill and sustain oneself, and according to Esther, "I'm not sure why it is, but I love food more than just about anything else." She associates the rich food with memories of her grandfather, who used to be head waiter at a country club and "by the age of nine I had developed a passionate taste for cold vichyssoise and caviar and anchovy paste." At the luncheon, Esther eats two plates of caviar, along with chicken and avocados stuffed with crabmeat. The food, which reminds her of childhood, is a source of comfort.

Comfort is something Esther increasingly needs. Earlier, before the banquet, she was reprimanded by Jay Cee, her boss and the editor of the magazine. Esther cries at the banquet when she recalls the scene. Jay Cee wants Esther to show more ambition. Esther admits,

> I felt very low. I had been unmasked only that morning by Jay Cee herself, and I felt now that all the uncomfortable suspicions I had about myself were coming true, and I couldn't hide the truth much longer. After nineteen years of running after good marks and prizes and grants of one sort and another, I was letting up, slowing down, dropping clean out of the race.

Esther feels disappointed in herself; her many scholastic achievements suddenly seem meaningless. In New York, her problems and worries mount and become increasingly impossible to ignore, as Bennett explains: "Esther discovers that the image on which she has depended for the first nineteen years of her life is a fraud" (125).

In Chapters 3 and 4, Esther begins to feel more directionless, confused, and inadequate. An accomplished young woman, she consistently earns the highest grades. She is writing her thesis on "twin images" in James Joyce's *Finnegans Wake* (a novel she has never actually finished). She is a college correspondent for the town *Gazette*, editor of the literary magazine, and secretary of the Honor Board. She has always been a model student, destined for great things, but suddenly her future seems muddled and unclear. For her entire academic career,

Esther has been striving for accomplishment, imagining that she would be a poet or a professor, but now she fears that her achievements will get her nowhere. When Jay Cee asks Esther what she wants to do after she graduates, she replies she doesn't know: "I felt a deep shock, hearing myself say that, because the minute I said it, I knew it was true."

Esther admires Jay Cee: She is smart, ambitious, and professional, offering an alternative to the happy homemaker. She is also stereotypically unattractive. Esther wishes "I had a mother like Jay Cee. Then I would know what to do. My own mother wasn't much help." Esther's mother, who emigrated from Germany as a child, teaches shorthand and typing in order to support her family, because Esther's father died when she was a child. She believes her mother secretly "hated him for dying and leaving no money." Esther's mother is proud of her daughter's accomplishments but wants her to do something practical. Although Esther admires Jay Cee, she also does not see herself following in her footsteps: Esther hates the magazine itself, and Jay Cee, in her view, has sacrificed her femininity for independence. Throughout the novel, various women advise Esther, and though she listens, she finds herself unable or unwilling to follow the particular paths they take.

At the banquet, Esther sits with Betsy. Doreen, spending "most of her time with Lenny Shepherd," is absent. When Esther finishes her meal, she uses the finger bowl and remembers a dinner with Philomena Guinea, the wealthy novelist who funds Esther's scholarship. In confusion, Esther had drunk the contents of the finger bowl, thinking it was a Japanese soup, a humorous incident that reveals her inexperience. These early chapters also portray Esther's financial insecurity: She has grown up poor and feels out of place in upscale restaurants, as she is only used to "Howard Johnson's." It is through the charity of others that she is able to go to school and spend a summer in New York; pressure to do well weighs heavily on her. Lacking purpose and motivation, she feels stuck; she cannot continue her hard work but also cannot, or will not, rebel: "I wondered why I couldn't go the whole way doing what I should any more. This made me sad and tired. Then I wondered why I couldn't go the whole way doing what I shouldn't, the way Doreen did, and this made me even sadder and more tired."

While Esther admires Doreen's rebelliousness, she feels she can never behave so freely and instead tries to emulate Betsy's wholesome image. Yet Esther is too sharp and cynical to wholly imitate Betsy's innocence, and soon she realizes that Betsy's respectability is also not necessarily a good model for her either. After the dinner, in Chapter 4, Esther, Betsy, and the other student interns go to a movie, a Hollywood Technicolor romance in which most of the action "took place in the football stands." The minor actresses resemble Hollywood stars, and the two main men are "boneheads." Esther figures out that "the nice girl was going to end up with the nice football hero and the sexy girl was going to end up with nobody." The "sexy girl" represents Doreen, who will end up empty-handed, while the good girl, reminiscent of Betsy, will be rewarded with marriage. Appropriately, it is at this point that Esther "began to feel peculiar." Feeling sick, Esther and Betsy leave together, and both throw up in the cab ride to the hotel, where Esther gets violently ill and passes out on the bathroom floor. The critic Tim Kendell links the food sickness with the film, both representing 1950s ideals about women: "The food which had looked good enough to photograph for the housewives of America is not good enough to eat. Esther discovers that the spotless hygiene of the 1950s technicolor America is a façade which may conceal an unhealthy reality—it may even make you sick" (53). The perfect homemaker is not real but an illusion, as is the stereotypical Hollywood romance, but both hold tremendous power over young women as dreams and realizable goals that they must strive to attain.

Esther and ten other student editors are sick from the crabmeat—discovered to be "chock-full of ptomaine." In the novel's early chapters, it is the body that is vulnerable and suffers the effects of taint and overindulgence (the crabmeat, Doreen's drunkenness) while the second half focuses on internal sickness (the poisoning of Esther's mind). Esther's vomiting, like the bathtub baptism, makes Esther feel "pure and holy and ready for a new life." Doreen, the only healthy one of the group, feeds her chicken noodle soup, and Esther soon feels rejuvenated and renewed.

**4**

The morning after her brief illness, in Chapter 5, Esther gets a phone call from Constantin, an interpreter at the United Nations and an acquaintance of Mrs. Willard's, Buddy's tweed-wearing mother. At this point, Esther has not yet broken up with Buddy, who is ill with tuberculosis and spending the summer in an upstate New York sanitarium. At one point, Esther worshipped him from afar, but now feels estranged from him: "although everybody still thought I would marry him . . . I knew I would never marry him if he were the last man on earth." Chapters 5 and 6 focus on her relationship with Buddy and her fear of marriage. Society expects her to find a nice, responsible young man and become his dutiful wife, but Esther has always gone after her own aspirations.

A story she reads in the book *The Thirty Best Short Stories of the Year*, given to her by the *Ladies' Day* magazine staff, triggers thoughts of Buddy. In this story, a Jewish man and a nun meet under a fig tree. One day, watching a chick being born, they touch hands, and the next day, the nun does not leave the convent. Esther draws parallels between this story and her relationship with Buddy, but while the fig tree nourishes the love of the couple, Esther's love for Buddy rots: "We had met together under our own imaginary fig tree, and what we had seen wasn't a bird coming out of an egg but a baby coming out of a woman, and then something awful happened and we went our separate ways."

Esther had a crush on Buddy for years, and then one day he stopped by her mother's house and said he would like to see her at college. Several months later he visited her but then said he was there to take Joan Gilling to a dance. Joan, who appears later in the novel, is first described as "a big-wheel president of her class and physics major and the college hockey champion." Esther lies and says she is going on a date, and Buddy, jealous, leaves. But he also gives her a letter, inviting Esther to the Yale junior prom, a proposal that leaves her excited and giddy.

Esther's glowing thoughts of Buddy, however, quickly darken. Buddy is studying to be a doctor, but instead of associating him with healing, Esther connects him to violence and the grotesque. In Chapter 6, Esther explains how Buddy took her on a tour of the hospital that is part of Yale Medical School. The tour included dissected cadavers and fetuses in glass jars. The two also watched a baby being born, a violent and painful scene, in which the mother had to be cut in order to free the baby. Esther was upset but said nothing to Buddy. She became even more upset when she learned that the woman was given drugs so she would not recall the pain: "I thought it sounded just like the sort of drug a man would invent. Here was a woman in terrible pain, obviously feeling every bit of it or she wouldn't groan like that, and she would go straight home and start another baby, because the drug would make her forget how bad the pain had been." This serves as an early example of the medical establishment's control over a woman's body, foreshadowing Esther's later experience with electroshock therapy. Her courtship with Buddy is marked with graphic imagery—the dissection of cadavers; the pickled, premature babies; and the bloody childbirth. Feeling pressured to act like a devoted, supportive girlfriend, though, Esther never lets on that she is disturbed.

Society and family view Buddy as the perfect man for her to marry: "My mother and my grandmother had started hinting around to me a lot lately about what a fine, clean boy Buddy Willard was, coming from such a fine, clean family, and how everybody at church thought he was a model person." But Esther is aware of Buddy's flaws: He dismisses her passion for literature, he patronizes her, and he does not want a woman who aspires to anything beyond her wifely duties. Esther fears the only real option for a woman is to be a wife and mother and thus to be in terrible pain. Esther is terrified of marriage and of sex, which underscores her reaction when she sees Buddy naked for the first time.

Back at his dorm room, Buddy asks Esther if she had ever seen a man naked before. He removes his clothes as if this were a medical duty, without any passion or love, and when he is naked, Esther admits, "The only thing I could think of was turkey neck and turkey gizzards," an image that "catches up all cocky masculine pride of flesh and reduces it to the level of giblets" (Scholes 132). Esther refuses his request for her to undress and instead asks Buddy if he has ever had sexual relations with anyone. During their courtship, Buddy has implied that he is sexually inexperienced, but now she questions his honesty.

Buddy admits to having a fling with a waitress at a summer job in Cape Cod, a confession that causes Esther to feel betrayed: "he had only been pretending all this time to be so innocent." It is not his affair with the woman that bothers Esther but that he presented himself as pure: "What I couldn't stand was Buddy's pretending I was so sexy and he was so pure, when all the time he'd been having an affair with that tarty waitress and must have felt like laughing in my face." Buddy is not only revealed not to be the model of a "fine, clean boy," but at the same time society is portrayed as allowing, even encouraging, him to engage in premarital sex. Esther balks at and rejects society's double standard, realizing "that Buddy can construct his own sexual identity while she cannot" (Badia 134). Buddy believes that Esther should be virginal and yet accepting of his affair. Esther decides to break up with him, but he later calls to tell her he has contracted tuberculosis, so she does not yet go through with it, causing her to feel "a wonderful relief. I thought the TB might just be a punishment for living the kind of double life Buddy lived and feeling so superior to people." Esther feels little compassion for Buddy, but she is good at playing the part of the concerned girlfriend and tells her friends they are practically engaged. Unclear about who exactly she is, Esther knows how she is supposed to act. For Buddy, she is the virginal girlfriend; for Jay Cee, the career girl; and for her mother, the studious, good daughter. But the more she acts, the more she loses touch with her essential, real self. The many conflicting identities she attempts to take on and expectations she tries to fulfill only contribute to her growing feelings of loss and confusion.

In chapter 7, Esther goes on a date with Constantin. Though he is "much too short," he is polite, kind, and smart, with a "lively, challenging expression." They quickly discover that neither of them likes Mrs. Willard. When Constantin grabs her hand, she feels "happier than I had been since I was about nine and running along the hot white beaches with my father the summer before he died." Esther suddenly thinks "how strange it had never occurred to me before that I was only truly happy until I was nine years old." Her father's death left a profound gap in her life. As a child, she did not question her identity or her happiness, but now, at the United Nations, the skills of the interpreters impress Esther and cause her to dwell on her perceived inadequacies. She realizes that her main achievement has been winning scholarships and fears the end of college will erase the identity she has so far established for herself. She thinks about all the "things I couldn't do." For example, she cannot cook and she does not know shorthand, both skills that society deemed necessary for young women. Her mother has told her to learn shorthand because then she "would be in demand among all the up-and-coming young men and she would transcribe letter after thrilling letter." But Esther "hated the idea of serving men in any way. I wanted to dictate my own thrilling letters."

As her feelings of inadequacy intensify, Esther feels paralyzed about the future: "I saw my life branching out before me like the green fig tree in the story." Each fig represents a particular role, such as wife, poet, professor, editor, or traveler: "I wanted each and every one of them, but choosing one meant losing all the rest, and, as I sat there unable to decide, the figs began to wrinkle and go black, and one by one, they plopped to the ground at my feet." She fears that each choice is exclusive; therefore, because she cannot choose only one, her future choices and options wither and languish. She feels enormous pressure to marry and start a family but also longs deeply to be independent—a writer and adventurer. She does not view these choices in a positive light but sees them as entrapments, as critic Janet Badia attests: "As her description of the withering figs makes clear, the problem is not that she lacks choices or even that none of the options appeals to her; the problem lies in her desire to have what society tells her is impossible, 'two mutually exclusive things at one and the same time'" (133).

As a young woman coming of age in the 1950s, Esther is trying to navigate her way through sex and womanhood. One may argue that Esther's belief that a married woman must give up her identity is naïve, yet this idea was heavily promoted by 1950s society: A woman must remain a virgin until marriage and then as a wife must submit herself to her husband's will and to furthering his success and livelihood. Mrs. Willard believes that a woman must support her husband's ambitions while silencing her own: "What a man is is an arrow into the future, and what a woman is is the place the arrow shoots off from." Esther rebels against this conventional notion but is unsure how to resist and reject such traditional gender roles, a state that only leads to insecurity and confusion. Critic Diane S. Bonds argues:

> The novel dramatizes a double bind for women in which, on the one hand, an authentic self is one that is presumed to be autonomous and whole, entire to itself and clearly bounded, and yet, in which, on the other hand, women have their identity primarily through relationship to a man. It is the increasing tension of this double bind for Esther which results in her breakdown. (61)

Her mother's only help on the subject is to give her a *Reader's Digest* article called "Defense of Chastity," which promotes Mrs. Willard's views that a woman must silence her own needs and wants in order to take care of her husband. The article also defends the sexual double standard that a woman must stay pure before marriage, but it is an optional requirement for men. After Buddy's disclosure, Esther now adamantly rejects this philosophy: "I couldn't stand the idea of a woman having to have a single pure life and a man being able to have a double life, one pure and one not." Though Esther is terrified of getting pregnant, she hesitantly begins to embrace the notion that virginity is unrealistic—even someone as seemingly clean-cut as Buddy is not a virgin. But society labels women who are not virgins to be fallen or ruined. Esther thinks about a boy she knew, Eric, who lost his virginity to a prostitute but was so repulsed by the experience that he decided he would never sleep with a woman he loved, separating sex from love. Esther seems to consider this perspective limiting and does not view sex as something repulsive, as Eric did. At the same time, she understands that her society divides women into the pure and impure. Esther also divides the world into "people who had slept with somebody and people who hadn't" and thinks that losing her virginity will help her reach a better sense of her self, another example of her youth and naiveté: "I thought a spectacular change would come over me the day I crossed the boundary line."

After dinner, Constantin invites Esther over to his apartment to listen to music, and she hopes this "could mean only one thing." She decides she will sleep with Constantin, wanting him to seduce her so she can rival Buddy when it comes to sexual experience. However, Constantin does not seem to be physically attracted to her. They fall asleep next to each other. It is a pleasant experience for her, until she imagines herself married to him: "It would mean getting up at seven and cooking him eggs and bacon and toast and coffee and dawdling about in my nightgown. . . . This seemed a dreary and wasted life for a girl with fifteen years of straight A's," she concludes, "but I knew that's what marriage was like." Esther fears that marriage will be the end of any sense of self, recalling the beautiful rug that Mrs. Willard braided and then used as a kitchen mat to be trampled on by her son and husband: "And I knew that in spite of all the roses and kisses and restaurant dinners a man showered on a woman before he married her, what he secretly wanted when the wedding service ended was for her to flatten out underneath his feet like Mrs. Willard's kitchen mat." For Esther, the kitchen mat is a powerful symbol of a wife's expected role in marriage. Esther recalls Buddy Willard telling her that after she had children, she would not want to write poems anymore. She decides that marriage would only ruin her ambitions and destroy her desire to write.

## 5

In Chapter 8, the narrative returns to the time when Esther visited Buddy at the sanitarium. Buddy's father, a kind, "boyish" man, drove her up to the Adirondacks, a trip in which she "grew gloomier and gloomier." Mr. Willard tells Esther that he and his wife always wanted a daughter, but "I don't see how any daughter could be nicer than you," another voice of support for Esther's and Buddy's marriage, which causes Esther to cry. Mr. Willard believes she is crying from joy, but it is actually because she feels trapped and does not know how to free herself from the situation she is in.

At the sanitarium, the color scheme is "based on liver." Throughout, Esther makes distinctive observations about colors, which usually depict the mood of the place or her perception of it. Buddy is now "fat." He proudly shows Esther a poem he published in a "thin, gray magazine." Though Buddy does not care about poetry—he says a poem is "nothing but a piece of dust"—he wants to prove to Esther that he can write as well as she can. She tells him it's "Not bad," though she "thought it was dreadful." Esther does not fail to notice that he signed his name B.S. Willard.

At the sanitarium, Buddy proposes to her, and Esther has "an awful impulse to laugh." She turns him down, and at first he assumes she is interested in another man, but then she tells him, "I'm never going to get married." Buddy is relieved; in his view, though, it is not possible that she will remain unmarried her entire life. He condescendingly insists she will change her mind. But Esther believes that Buddy wants her to choose between being a writer and becoming a mother. She understands that she could never fit into one mold: "If neurotic is wanting two mutually exclusive things at one and the same time, then I'm neurotic as hell."

Turning down Buddy's proposal marks a defining moment for Esther in asserting her will and identity and in taking charge of her life, but she does not know where to go from here. She has rejected the conventional path, but where does that leave her? Later that day, Buddy, who still seems unconvinced that they will not get married, decides he will teach Esther how to ski, even though he has only been a few times himself. Though Esther has never skied before, "It never occurred to me to say no." As she stands on the hill, the image of the sky reflects her loneliness: "The great, gray eye of the sky looked back at me, its mist-shrouded sun focusing all the white and silent distances that poured from every point of the compass, hill after pale hill, to stall at my feet." She then sees Buddy waiting for her halfway down the hill. At first she is terrified, but then she thinks that maybe she will inevitably kill herself: "I . . . pushed myself into a flight I knew I couldn't stop by skill or any belated access of will" and plunges down the hill, "through year after year of doubleness and smiles and compromise, into my own past." She is happy, skiing into her past and hurtling toward possible death. She sees the near-death experience as a rite of purity and becomes upset only when reality returns. Critic Caroline King Barnard sees this wild plunge down the ski slope as a reaction to her refusal of Buddy's proposal:

> Buddy Willard's proposal of marriage places Esther in a particularly critical position, especially since her refusal expresses a rebellion she is not equipped to handle. Skiing with Buddy shortly thereafter, then, she again seeks to rid herself of her present world with its intolerable pressures and demands; this time her need is so great that even the death of her physical body is of no consequence. (29)

When a man steps into her path, she crashes and her mouth fills with ice. Determined, she wants to ski down the mountain again, but Buddy tells her, with a strange satisfaction, that her leg is "broken in two places. You'll be stuck in a cast for months," as if she is being punished for refusing to comply with the traditional path of marriage.

Until Chapter 9, Esther could be described as cynical, somewhat rebellious, but also fairly stable. When the narrative switches back to New York in Chapter 9, Esther's behavior becomes more erratic, and she begins to lose her ability to negotiate reality. The chapter opens at the cafeteria of the Amazon, where Esther is sitting with Hilda, another guest editor. Esther tries to make conversation by bringing up the Rosenbergs, who are to be executed that night. Instead of agreeing with Esther about how awful the execution is, Hilda says, "I'm so glad they're going to die." The reference to the Rosenbergs is symbolic of Esther's worry, anxiety, and unhappiness; their death symbolizes for her the ruthlessness of an unjust, uncaring world. Hilda's statement exemplifies how Esther feels disconnected from conventional society's viewpoints, a stance that only deepens her feelings of alienation.

Later, in a photo shoot for the magazine, Esther holds a paper rose meant to symbolize her desire to become a poet, and when the photographer tells her to smile, she bursts into tears: "When I lifted my head, the photographer had vanished. Jay Cee had vanished as well. I felt limp and betrayed, like the skin shed by a terrible animal." At this point, Esther's only hope is that, on her return to Massachusetts, she will be able to take the summer writing class taught by a famous writer that she applied to: "I was sure I'd find the letter of acceptance waiting on the mail table at home."

On Esther's last night in New York, Doreen persuades her to go to a country club dance with Lenny and a blind date, a friend of Lenny's. Marco is a Peruvian who gives Esther a diamond pin that she admires, but "the diamond stickpin is a signifier for marriage rights" (Boyer 208). The pin "dazzled and danced with light like a heavenly ice cube," but Marco roughly grabs her arm and says he will perform "some small service worthy of a diamond." Sadistic and controlling, Marco leaves four bruises on her arm, and Esther realizes he is "a woman-hater." Nonetheless, as if resigned to this danger, she stays with him. Critic Linda W. Wagner argues, "But even though the men in Esther's life are responsible for these events, Plath shows clearly that Esther's passivity and her lack of questioning are also responsible. Esther's malaise has made her incapable of dealing with aggression either subtle or overt—except privately" (60).

Marco insists that Esther tango with him, treating her like a rag doll: "Pretend you are drowning." After the dance, he leads her outside to the empty golf course. Esther asks him who he loves, and he tells her that he loves his cousin but that she is going to be a nun. Marco, like Eric and Buddy, categorizes women as pure or impure. Suddenly, full of anger, he pushes Esther down into the mud, climbs on top of her, and rips her dress. He tries to rape her, calling her a slut. At first, Esther is paralyzed, but then she fights back, smashing his nose. Terrified, she starts to cry. Marco smears her cheeks with the blood, leaving her marked, signifying her injury and submission and his power over her.

When she returns to the Amazon, Esther takes her bundle of New York clothes, climbs onto the roof, and throws her entire city wardrobe off, piece by piece: "like a loved one's ashes, the gray scraps were ferried off, to settle here, there, exactly where I would never know, into the dark heart of New York." She does not think about the practical considerations—that she will need clothes for the next day; rather the symbolism of the impetuous action prevails, a shedding of her New York experience. She throws away the clothes as if disposing of the last shreds of her identity and finally relinquishing her tenuous grasp of reality.

### 6

The next part of the novel is set in the suburbs, at her mother's house, where Esther grows increasingly troubled. In Chapter 10 she leaves New York, her behavior becoming more erratic. On the train ride home she is wearing one of Betsy's skirts and blouses because she did not think to save any of her own clothes. In her suitcase, instead of clothes, she carries "two dozen avocado pears." But the most disturbing aspect is that she has not washed Marco's blood off her face, proudly wearing the blood streaks "like the relic of a dead lover." Esther does not seem to understand why people are looking at her, a sign of her growing inability to discern reality.

When Esther arrives, "I stepped from the air-conditioned compartment onto the station platform, and the motherly breath of the suburbs enfolded me. It smelt of lawn sprinklers and station wagons and tennis rackets and dogs and babies." She adds, "A summer calm laid its soothing hand over everything, like death." The suburbs then are the land of mothers and babies, suffocation and death, and, she fears, her future. Esther's mother is waiting for her at the station and immediately serves Esther bad news, "you didn't make that writing course," stripping away Esther's only hope for the summer. This disappointing development, which Esther sees as a personal defeat, precipitates her breakdown. Esther has always been good at winning academic prizes, and her achievements have defined her life, but now such a "blow destroys the last shred of self image (Greenwood as writer), and the second half of the novel shows Esther's education not in the process of becoming adult but rather in the process of becoming mad" (Wagner 61). The novel no longer reflects the traditional elements of the coming-of-age narrative but documents instead her descent into mental illness.

Stuck in the suburbs, Esther plunges deeper into depression. From her window, she watches her neighbor Dodo Conway with her six kids, a seventh on the way, and thinks, "Children made me sick." Her fears of motherhood and domesticity are now reinforced by the images drawn from her immediate environs. Wagner suggests that the image of Dodo Conway "brings all the scattered images of childbirth and female responsibility to a climax. Unless she accepts this role, Esther will have no life—this is the message her society, even the most supportive elements in it, gives her" (61).

When Jody, her college roommate, calls, Esther hears a "hollow voice," which is her own, explaining that she has decided to stay home for the summer. This moment, in which she hears herself speak, marks an even further development in her process of self-detachment. Immediately she feels torn by regret: "The minute I hung up I knew I should have said I would come. One morning listening to Dodo Conway's baby carriage would drive me crazy. And I made a point of never living in the same house with my mother for more than a week." After getting off the phone with Jody, Esther opens a letter from Buddy, in which he reveals that he has fallen in love with a nurse. He suggests that if Esther comes to the Adirondacks for the summer "he might well find his feeling for the nurse was mere infatuation." Furiously, Esther crosses out his words and writes back that she is "engaged to a simultaneous interpreter."

Esther's fear and uncertainty of the future are intensified after her rejection from the writing class. Throughout chapter 10, she flounders as she attempts to construct and envision a future: "I saw the years of my life spaced along a road in the form of telephone poles, threaded together by wires. I counted one, two, three . . . nineteen telephone poles, and then the wires dangled into space, and try as I would, I couldn't see a single pole beyond the nineteenth." This confession reveals her fear that there is no future for her and foreshadows her attempt to end her life. In vain, she tries desperately to invent a future for herself, another telephone pole. She decides she will write a novel but then abandons the idea, frustrated by her lack of life experience. Esther then agrees to let her mother teach her shorthand, but she does not actually want a job that requires knowledge of that particular skill. When Esther tries to read *Finnegans Wake*, the words dance and slide across the page, and she considers dropping her thesis and transferring out of the honors program, until she realizes she would have to take too many literature classes: "I hated the very idea of the eighteenth century, with all those smug men writing tight little couplets and being so dead keen on reason." Esther also contemplates dropping out of school to be a waitress or a typist, but "I couldn't stand the idea of being either one." As she frantically considers the spectrum of possibilities, she quickly rejects each one.

Overwhelmed, listless and detached, Esther cannot read or write. She does not bother to get dressed and has trouble sleeping. Not only must she live in her mother's house, but her mother sleeps in the same room with her, only adding to her suffocation. When her mother snores, she thinks "the only way to stop it would be to take the column of skin and sinew from which it rose and twist it to silence between my hands." Malaise, depression, and ennui become more deeply rooted in her. Toward the end of chapter 10, gaps and periods of unaccounted time break up the structure, as the reader eventually realizes that Esther is taking sleeping pills.

In chapters 11 and 12, Esther's illness becomes more severe. These chapters also give voice to her increasing distrust of the medical establishment, a view that is first established in chapter 6, when Buddy gave her the tour. In chapter 11, Esther visits Dr. Gordon, a psychiatrist. His waiting room is "hushed and beige." Beige is dull but also "safe." In this chapter, the reader learns more details about Esther's breakdown: She has not washed her clothes or hair in three weeks "because it seemed so silly." There is no point to anything because people "only died in the end." Now when she thinks about the future she sees

> the days of the year stretching ahead like a series of bright, white boxes, and separating one box from another was sleep, like a black shade. Only for me, the long perspective of shades that set off one box from the next had suddenly snapped up, and I could see day after day after day glaring ahead of me like a white, broad, infinitely desolate avenue.

The infinity and blankness of the future overwhelm her to the point of inducing paralysis.

She hopes that Dr. Gordon will help her, but she immediately distrusts him: "I hated him the minute I walked in through the door." Dr. Gordon is handsome, young, and conceited. He displays a picture of his wife and children on his desk, which Esther believes he puts there to ward off her advances. Esther seems to be increasingly paranoid and unreliable in her perception of reality, yet the reader also observes Dr. Gordon's insensitivity. Esther was hoping for a "kind, ugly, intuitive man" who "would help me, step by step, to be myself again." Esther wants to get help, but she cannot do so from Dr. Gordon, who symbolizes the patriarchal power of the medical establishment. Dr. Gordon does not seem interested in Esther's symptoms. He barely talks to her, except to comment on how pretty the girls at her college were when he worked there during the war. He wants to continue seeing Esther, which disappoints her mother, since he charges $25 an hour. Her mother does not understand Esther but loves her and wants her to get better.

Despite efforts to reverse her condition, Esther continues to lose touch with reality. When a sailor approaches her on the Boston Common, she flirts with him under the guise of her alter ego, Elly Higginbottom, an orphan from Chicago. Elly is her other, her double—more flirtatious and socially confident. Growing up as an orphan, Elly does not feel burdened by family pressures or expectations. Then Esther mistakenly thinks she sees Mrs. Willard. When she realizes the woman is not Mrs. Willard, she tells the sailor that this woman worked at the orphanage. When he asks if she was mean to Esther, she assents and starts to cry, convincing herself that this woman was "responsible for everything bad that happened" in her life.

Esther feels that she has taken "the wrong turn here and the wrong path there" but does not know how to make things right. She continues to see Dr. Gordon, though she feels nothing is gained or accomplished by the visits. Instead, she feels drawn toward death and begins collecting articles on suicides. As Linda W. Wagner points out, "Even during the second half of the novel, Esther remains the good student. In her study of suicide, she reads, asks questions, correlates material, chooses according to her own personality, and progresses just as if she were writing a term paper" (62). Esther is increasingly mocking and caustic; her sardonic narration functions as a way of protecting herself behind an impenetrable wall.

In Chapter 12, Esther undergoes electroshock therapy at Dr. Gordon's private hospital, an experience that only serves to increase her paranoia and collapse of perspective. When she arrives at the hospital, she is surprised to see that the patients look fairly normal. The living room is "the replica of a lounge in a guest house I visited once on an island off the coast of Maine." She observes that patients "in summer clothes were sitting about at card tables." But on closer examination, she realizes that none of the patients is "moving" and that they are like "shop dummies, painted to resemble people and propped up in attitudes counterfeiting life," reinforcing the notion that the medical establishment views mental illness as something to be hidden, controlled, and sanitized but not to be discussed, understood, or cured.

Dr. Gordon, in a position of power, does not explain what he is doing to Esther as he sets up the equipment. After, he makes the same comment about the pretty girls, which shows that he has not really been listening to her. He does not want to understand her suffering but wants to mold her into one of the "shop dummies" instead. He fits the metal plates on either side of her head, buckles them into place, and gives her a wire to bite; the mechanical, detached scene depicts the power of doctors over a female patient, which Esther witnessed on her tour with Buddy. Esther is terrified, as something "took hold of me and shook me like the end of the world." Esther believes she is being punished: "I wondered what terrible thing it was that I had done." The electrotherapy episode connects to the opening of the novel, when she expressed fear of electrocution. The motif of the Rosenbergs, according to Caroline King Barnard, is especially clear after her electroshock treatment:

> The Rosenbergs, possibly innocent, but helpless before the judgment of their accusers, have been put to death by electrocution. Esther instinctively equates their experience with her own; like the Rosenbergs, she feels powerless and victimized, threatened and judged by everyone and everything. (27)

The electric shock is a symbol of power and death; Esther associates this form of therapy with punishment, a kind of sentencing.

After the treatment, Esther tells her mother that she will not be going back to Dr. Gordon. Her mother is relieved: "I knew you'd decide to be all right again." Her mother's intentions are good, but she is in denial and thinks of her daughter's illness as a passing phase. Despite Esther's mental breakdown, she still attempts to maintain control of her body, and she fully understands that the doctor will not or cannot help her. Thus, both the medical establishment and her mother have failed her, and now Esther is determined to find her own cure. In her distorted view, the only cure is death. Focused on various images of death and suicide, she does not dwell on why she wants to kill herself but how, which she describes in a lucid, logical voice.

Esther compares herself to a picture of a starlet who died after lingering in a coma; their eyes have the same "dead, black, vacant expression." When Esther tries to slit her wrists, she cannot bring herself to pierce the skin: "what I wanted to kill wasn't in that skin or the thin blue pulse that jumped under my thumb, but somewhere else, deeper, more secret, a whole lot harder to get at." Extinguishing life in her physical body will not provide the satisfaction she craves, yet she feels she has no other options. She takes a bus to Deer Island Prison, near her childhood home, and plans to kill herself with razors, but then "I thought how stupid I was. I had the razors, but no warm bath." She stands on the beach, contemplating death, but when the waves hit her, her "flesh winced, in cowardice, from such a death." It is her mind she wants to escape, but she does not know how to enact this release without ending her physical existence. The calm, detached first-person voice convinces the reader that her ideas are somewhat rational, allowing the reader to closely follow the path and course of her breakdown.

## 7

Esther's desire to end her life—in order to stop her mental suffering—intensifies, even though she masks this desire when around others, attempting to act stable and normal around others. In Chapter 13, Esther goes to the beach with her college friend Jody, Jody's boyfriend, and Cal. The presence of the handsome Cal causes Esther to wonder "if I'd been my old self, if I would have liked him." They discuss a play in which a mother considers killing her son because he is mentally ill, a play that Esther remembers because "everything I had ever read about mad people stuck in my mind, while everything else flew out." This scene depicts how detached Esther is from her friends and their lighthearted concerns; instead of enjoying a carefree day at the beach, she is obsessed with thoughts of death. Though she tries to pretend she is fine, she is afraid "at any moment my control would snap." Unable to keep her thoughts of death at bay, she asks Cal, if he decided to kill himself, how would he do it? Cal replies that he would shoot himself in the head, and Esther is disappointed: "It was just like a man to do it with a gun. A fat chance I had of laying my hands on a gun." Then Esther challenges Cal to swim out to a rock, thinking that "drowning must be the kindest way to die, and burning the worst." Cal follows for a while, then stops, out of breath, and heads back to shore. Esther continues swimming toward her death, "my heartbeat boomed like a dull motor in my ears. I am I am I am."

To stop this "I am" earlier that morning, Esther tried to use the silk cord of her mother's yellow bathrobe to hang herself, but she explains how "each time I would get the cord so tight I could feel a rushing in my ears and a flush of blood in my face, my hands would weaken and let go, and I would be all right again." Her body is stronger than her mind in its desire to live. Swimming across the water, she realizes that the rock is too far away and worries that, by the time she reaches it, she will be too tired to jump from it. She reasons, "The only thing to do was to drown myself then and there." However, again, her body fights her will to die: "I dived, and dived again, and each time popped up like a cork." Finally, "beaten" she gives up and swims back to shore.

Though death-obsessed, Esther still would like to get help, thinking that she could go "into an asylum where I could be cured." Yet she fears that an asylum would mean "Doctor Gordon and his private shock machine." In the face of that option, Esther would rather choose death. She also realizes her family could never afford that kind of care. The studious young woman that she is, Esther has been reading up on abnormal psychology. She understands what is happening to her and fears that she is incurable.

Esther's mother, however, believes the illness is a temporary phase and convinces Esther that volunteering will help pull her out of depression. So Esther volunteers at a hospital, and on the first day, she must deliver flowers to the women who have just given birth. She obsesses over the dead flowers and rearranges the bouquets, angering the new mothers. Overwhelmed and panicked, Esther runs off. She considers other options, such as becoming Catholic, thinking she would be talked out of suicide, a sin, and then wonders if she could become a nun, so that it would "take up the whole of [her] life." Her mother laughs at this idea.

In Chapter 13, Esther visits her father's grave: "I thought it odd that in all the time my father had been buried in this graveyard, none of us had ever visited him." She searches for his grave, feeling "a great yearning, lately, to pay my father back for all the years of neglect." The "fine drizzle started drifting down from the gray sky," and Esther sits on the grass of her father's grave and cries. Esther's father died when she was nine, and she realizes "I had never cried." His death never seemed real to her because she did not cry, following her mother's example.

Several external factors have contributed to Esther's despair, including the death of her father; the darkness she perceives as inherent to life and society (such as the execution of the Rosenbergs); and her troubling, often violent, experiences with men. But none of these obstacles or perceptual distortions is impossible to overcome. Plath suggests that Esther's suicide attempts are the result of a mental illness, that her own tortured mind alone drives her to kill herself. On the other hand, external factors play a major part in her breakdown, specifically in terms of the pressure she feels from society. As Diane Bonds suggests: "the novel makes it sufficiently clear that she is torn apart by the intolerable conflict between her wish to avoid domesticity, marriage and motherhood, on the one hand, and her inability to conceive of a viable future in which she avoids that fate, on the other" (54).

After her several suicide attempts, which she always abandons out of fear or for attempting an impractical means, in Chapter 13 Esther writes her mother a note to tell her she is going on a long walk. She then retrieves her sleeping pills from her mother's lockbox and goes to the cellar, where she swallows 50 of them. At first, the reader does not realize that she is serious; nothing in her calm, unwavering matter-of-fact tone indicates that this time will be different. The reader nearly forgets that she is doing something as momentous as taking her life:

> At first nothing happened but as I approached the bottom of the bottle, red and blue lights began to flash before my eyes. The bottle slid from my fingers and I lay down. The silence drew off, baring the pebbles and shells and all the tatty wreckage of my life. Then, at the rim of vision, it gathered itself, and in one sweeping tide, rushed me to sleep.

The crawlspace that she chooses to die in is symbolic of a womb—in her search for death, she hopes for rebirth. Yet she is closer to decay than renewal, as "Cobwebs touched my face."

Chapter 14 continues with Esther in the cellar, drugged by the sleeping pills. When she wakes, semiconscious, in darkness, there is a chisel of light chipping away the dark: "Then the chisel struck again, and the light leapt into my head, and through the thick, warm, furry dark, a voice cried, 'mother!'" The voice, of course, is her own—and now, wanting to leave the "womb," she calls for her mother.

Esther wakes up in a hospital feeling hopeless: Nothing has changed. She is in despair at her situation and now even more paranoid. She feels like a medical test case, to be looked at and studied. She is visited by her mother, who wears a "dress with purple cartwheels on it," and her brother, back from Germany. She is also visited by a college acquaintance, a young man who she tells to leave because "He just wanted to see what a girl who was crazy enough to kill herself looked like." At this point, Esther seems to be through with acting or pretending to be someone she is not. When her brother asks her how she is, she looks her mother "in the eye" and says, "The same."

Much to the objection of the nurse, Esther looks in a mirror, and at first does not believe the reflection is hers:

You couldn't tell whether the person in the picture was a man or a woman, because their hair was shaved off and sprouted in bristly chicken-feather tufts all over their head. One side of the person's face was purple, and bulged out in a shapeless way, shading to green along the edges, and then to a sallow yellow. The person's mouth was pale brown, with a rose-colored sore at either corner.

Reflections and faces haunt Esther throughout the narrative, symbolizing her disconnected identities. In this reflection, she is disfigured; her mental desperation is symbolized by the horror of her face. When she realizes she is looking at herself, she breaks the mirror, and after this outburst, she is transferred to "a special ward" in the city hospital.

There, in the psychiatric ward, her paranoia increases. When she and her mother are in the garden, she believes another patient, Mrs. Tomolillo, is imitating every move her mother makes. She also feels certain the doctors give out fake names and write down whatever she says. When one of the aides serves two kinds of beans with dinner, Esther thinks he is trying to mock the patients. She speaks to him in a bossy way and he replies, calling her "Miss Mucky-Muck." As Kate Baldwin points out, he is a character who "reads Esther accurately" (34). Before the dinner is over, Esther kicks the aide in the leg. While a victim of herself and her self-loathing, Esther's flaws and prejudices are many. She expresses racism and, later, homophobia and exhibits an unshakable sense of entitlement yet still remains a sympathetic narrator despite the negative qualities and behaviors she displays. Feeling trapped, she expresses her anger and sense of entrapment by smashing a stack of thermometers. Before the nurse wheels her out, she scoops up a ball of mercury, which symbolizes her need to find a way to mend the disconnected parts of herself: "I opened my fingers a crack, like a child with a secret, and smiled at the silver globe cupped in my palm. If I dropped it, it would break into a million little replicas of itself, and if I pushed them near each other, they would fuse, without a crack, into one whole again."

## 8

In Chapter 15, after asking her mother to have her discharged from the asylum, Esther leaves the city hospital to enter a private one, where the expenses are being paid by Philomena Guinea, the sponsor of Esther's college scholarship: "Philomena Guinea was buying my freedom." During the peak of her writing career, Guinea had apparently also been in an asylum. When she read about Esther in a Boston newspaper, Guinea telegrammed Esther's mother saying that she would help, but not if a boy was involved. Her mother telegrammed back, "No, it is Esther's writing. She thinks she will never write again." In response, Guinea flies to Boston to drive Esther to the posh private hospital. Esther thinks she should feel grateful, but she feels numb. She fears that the hospital will not be able to help, that "wherever I sat—on the deck of a ship or at a street café in Paris or Bangkok—I would be sitting under the same glass bell jar, stewing in my own sour air." A bell jar is an archaic laboratory tool, an airtight, dust-free jar used for displaying specimens. Esther feels trapped in the bell jar, separated from the world of the living. She has trouble empathizing with others because she cannot escape the confines of her own mental and psychological world. She also feels as if she is being constantly watched by those around her. Critic Howard Moss adds, "Esther is cut off from the instinct for sympathy right from the beginning—for herself as well as for others. . . . A thin layer of glass separates her from everyone" (178).

The differences between the private hospital and the city one are numerous. The private hospital, with its beautiful grounds, resembles a country club. The patients dine off white linen tablecloths and drink from glasses, as opposed to the city hospital where "we had drunk out of paper cups and had no knives to cut our meat." When Esther arrives, the other patients are outside, playing badminton and golf, and Esther worries that she is the only one who is sick.

Another significant difference is that Esther now has a female psychiatrist: "I was surprised to have a woman. I didn't think they had woman psychiatrists." Dr. Nolan challenges the predominate view of the 1950s that only men could be doctors. Sophisticated, smart, and gentle, Dr. Nolan helps lead Esther on a path to healing. In their first meeting, she surprises Esther by asking if she liked Dr. Gordon: "I thought the doctors must all be in it together." When Esther tells her the truth about the electroshock therapy, "blue flashes, and the jolting and the noise," Dr. Nolan looks upset, and she tells Esther that electroshock therapy should feel like going to sleep and that some people actually like it. Esther warns if she has any more shock treatments, she will kill herself, and Dr. Nolan promises her that if she needs to undergo it again, "it won't be anything like what you had before."

The description of the surroundings and of Dr. Nolan add an element of hope to the narrative, suggesting that the lid of the bell jar might possibly be lifted, yet at this point, Esther sees no viable or positive changes in herself. She receives injections and insulin, but "I never seemed to get any reaction. I just grew fatter and fatter." After a short time there, she receives walking privileges, and she is no longer death obsessed. Esther's tone, however, continues to be caustic, mocking, and nonchalant.

The private hospital consists of three wards. Belsize is where the patients who will soon be released stay. Caplan, where Esther starts out, is a middle ground, and Wymark is for those patients who will not improve, such as Mrs. Norris, who does not speak. Before the silent Mrs. Norris is transferred, Esther sits with her at dinner, enjoying her company. Though the level of patient care is far superior at the private hospital, it still serves as an illuminating example of the way the medical establishment exerts power over "sick" women: The women are analyzed, medicated, and operated on according to how rebellious, hysterical, or troubled they are. For example, while at Caplan, Esther meets a friendly girl named Valerie, who shows Esther the scars from her lobotomy. Valerie used to be angry, but now she feels fine and shows no desire to leave the hospital to rejoin society.

At the end of chapter 15, Esther moves into a sunnier room, and Joan Gilling, an acquaintance from college whom Buddy had dated before Esther, checks in. Chapter 16 focuses on Joan, who tells Esther that she read about her suicide attempt in the newspaper and tried to emulate her. Joan reveals the scars on her wrists where she smashed her hands through a window. Esther expresses no sympathy for Joan and yet seems interested in her and her case. Joan has saved all of the clippings about Esther's suicide attempt, incorporating specific details about it into the narrative. First, her mother reported her missing and later discovered that the pills were gone. A search party, including police with dogs, looked for her until the third day, when her mother was in the basement doing laundry and heard a whimpering coming from the crawlspace: "The last picture shows policemen lifting a long, limp blanket roll with a featureless cabbage head into the back of an ambulance."

Dr. Nolan decides that Esther should not have any more visitors, and Esther is pleased: "Why that's wonderful." The visits diminish her sense of self-worth and make her especially sensitive to her current situation. She feels she is being viewed and evaluated in terms of the all-American girl she once was, which is yet another way she feels pressured to conform to a societal ideal: "I hated these visits, because I kept feeling the visitors measuring my fat and stringy hair against what I had been and what they wanted me to be, and I knew they went away utterly confounded." At this point in the narrative, she no longer pretends to be the perfect young woman and daughter. Though her mother loves her, she only adds to Esther's feelings of inadequacy: "My mother was the worst. She never scolded me, but kept begging me, with a sorrowful face, to tell her what she had done wrong." Esther tells Dr. Nolan that, earlier that day, her mother had brought her roses for her birthday, and Esther had said, "Save them for my funeral." She tells Dr. Nolan, "I hate her." Esther expects that Dr. Nolan will express shock or dismay by this revelation, but instead Dr. Nolan smiles: "I suppose you do." On the one hand, Esther, having read the clippings, knows how worried and scared her mother was in the wake of her daughter's suicide attempt and yet she does not seem to care what her mother went through, behaving cruelly and coldly to her, unwilling to recognize or take responsibility for the suffering her own actions have caused. On the other hand, her mother makes Esther feel guilty for not being the perfect daughter, and this is one of the first times in which she expresses her anger. Because she is able to honestly confront her feelings, she grows more confident, which in turn furthers her recovery. Dr. Nolan, by listening to Esther and validating her feelings, slowly builds Esther's trust of doctors.

## 9

Esther is transferred to Belsize in Chapter 17. The patients there seem to behave quite normally—playing bridge, singing around a piano, and gossiping. Joan Gilling is also at Belsize, but now Esther feels that Joan is treating her coolly. She and Joan engage in a push-pull relationship. Now that Joan seems to be recovering, Esther worries that she herself is sick: "Joan was the beaming double of my old best self, especially designed to follow and torment me."

This fear seems to be confirmed one morning when the nurse does not bring Esther her breakfast tray. Terrified that this means she is to undergo shock therapy, Esther hides in the hall and weeps, feeling betrayed by Dr. Nolan: "It wasn't the shock treatment that struck me, as much as the bare-faced treachery of Doctor Nolan. I liked Doctor Nolan, I loved her." Esther's trust in Dr. Nolan has been compromised, until Dr. Nolan finds her, "hugged me like a mother," and explains that she did not warn Esther about the electroshock therapy the night before because she did not want her to worry. Dr. Nolan is the only character in the novel whom Esther claims to love and trust entirely. When Dr. Nolan promises to stay by her side during the procedure, Esther relents, and Dr. Nolan "hooked her arm in my arm, like an old friend." During the session, Miss Huey talks to Esther in a "low, soothing voice," and this time when the shock is administered "darkness wiped me out like chalk on a blackboard."

In Chapter 18, Esther wakes up from the electroshock therapy to find Dr. Nolan with her. She feels "surprisingly at peace. The bell jar hung, suspended, a few feet above my head. I was open to the circulating air." Her thoughts of violence and suicide dissipate, as indicated when she holds a knife but can no longer remember her attraction to knives. Critic Robert Scholes explains, "Ironically, that same electrical power which destroys the Rosenbergs restores Esther to life. It is shock therapy which finally lifts the bell jar and enables Esther to breathe freely once again" (131). Most likely, the combination of the insulin treatment, counseling, and shock therapy (still standard treatment for mental illness at the time) helps her to improve. But Kate A. Baldwin questions if this "rebirth" image is so positive: "Esther's rebirth by electroconvulsive shock therapy (ECT) is, however, undercut by the multiple gaps the text summons: we are left with the uncanny sense of suspension. Readers are left to wonder about that space between the novel's end and the writing of the narrative from that location of health and recovery" (25).

Both Joan and Esther receive letters from Buddy, who wants to visit them. Esther tires easily of Joan, who "hung about me like a large and breathless fruit fly—as if the sweetness of recovery were something she could suck up by mere nearness." The two of them continue their reciprocal relationship: As Esther is getting better, Joan's mental health declines. Yet Esther also feels drawn to Joan: "In spite of the creepy feeling, and in spite of my old, ingrained dislike, Joan fascinated me. It was like observing a Martian, or a particularly warty toad." She considers Joan to be her double: "Her thoughts were not my thoughts, nor her feelings my feelings, but we were close enough so that her thoughts and feelings seemed a wry, black image of my own. Sometimes I wondered if I had made Joan up." Following the novel's themes of twins and doubles, Joan represents Esther's twin, a part of Esther's fractured self.

Esther behaves cruelly toward Joan after she walks in on Joan and Dee Dee, another patient, in bed together. The incident causes her to remember two lesbians from college. She expresses a curiosity about lesbian desire and asks Dr. Nolan what women see in other women, to which Dr. Nolan responds, "Tenderness." Esther seems to seriously consider this reply, but around Joan, her homophobia prevails, and she lashes out. When Joan tells her, "I like you better than Buddy," Esther responds: "I don't like you. You make me puke, if you want to know." Esther ruins any chances at establishing an emotional bond with another woman, except in her therapy sessions with Dr. Nolan. Esther can be starkly dismissive of others and often resorts to stereotypes when describing other women.

Esther is sorting out her feelings about men, about losing her virginity, and about her fear of pregnancy. To separate herself from Joan (and to be a part of the 1950s ideal of what was considered normal), Esther must assert her heterosexual identity, though as Bonds reminds us, "it should be noted that her encounters with men have been nearly devastating" (59). When Esther tells Dr. Nolan about the *Reader's Digest* article her mother gave her, Dr. Nolan laughs and calls it "propaganda." Following Dr. Nolan's recommendation, Esther gets fitted for a diaphragm, a birth-control device, freeing her from the possibility of pregnancy: "I was my own woman. The next step was to find the proper sort of man." This is the moment in which Esther gains her independence, Bennett asserts:

> Her dilemma is resolved, however factitiously, in the final section of the novel through her contact with Dr. Nolan, the "good mother," and through her acquisition of a diaphragm, the contraceptive device that will presumably allow her to exercise her femininity without fear of accidentally falling under the domination of a man by becoming pregnant and therefore dependent, as, in effect, Plath's mother did. (125)

Birth control was illegal in Massachusetts at the time, so it is only with Dr. Nolan's help that she is able to see a doctor who fits her for a diaphragm. Yet Esther is mistaken to think that sex will give her back her identity or that this will free her from her struggle. Bennett questions whether this sexual freedom leads to a real change in Esther: "Dr. Nolan is able to free the princess from the spell that holds her bound, immobilized, in place. But the sad fact is that the wand she uses is a diaphragm. Into Esther's otherwise unchanged hands, she places the instrument meant to secure Esther's sexuality while releasing her from the paralyzing fear of its consequences" (129). Yet Esther views losing her virginity, without the fear of getting pregnant, as a sign of freedom and independence.

## 10

In the final two chapters, Esther edges closer to recovery. In Chapter 19, Joan is also better and released from Belsize to live with a nurse in Cambridge; she tells Esther that she wants to become a psychiatrist. Instead of feeling happy for Joan, Esther is jealous, although she will also be leaving soon and returning to school. Her doctors, however, insist that she stay through the winter break at the asylum and "vetoed my living with my mother in the interim."

Esther meets Irwin, a math professor, on the steps of Widener Library and decides to sleep with him. She chooses him because he seems intelligent and experienced and because he is a stranger. After a couple of dates, she goes to his apartment, and they sleep together. Though she loses her virginity, she is not transformed as she had expected: "all I felt was a sharp, startlingly bad pain." Esther starts bleeding badly, but Irwin does not seem concerned. Esther recalls stories about virgins bleeding on their wedding night; the situation also recalls the earlier scene when Marco streaked her face with his blood, marking her. Esther instructs Irwin to drive her to Joan's. Though Esther is not honest with her about the cause of the bleeding, Joan serves as her nurse. She calls the hospital and rides with Esther in the taxi. At the emergency room, the doctor "whistled" at the amount of blood loss, telling her "it's one in a million it happens to like this." Despite the pain, Esther seems pleased that she took control of her sexuality. She has put her mother and Mrs. Willard out of her mind and also no longer needs to summon her alternate persona, Elly Higginbottom. Yet as Wagner points out:

Her aggression in finding Irwin so that she can be sexually experienced is a positive sign, but the characteristic irony—that she be the one in a million to hemorrhage after intercourse—mars the experience and tends to foreshadow the incipient bad luck which may follow cultural role reversal. As Plath knew only too well, society had its ways of punishing women who were too aggressive, too competent, and too masculine. (66)

A few day later, Joan returns to Belsize. Esther does not offer any explanation or thoughts on her return, wondering instead if Dr. Quinn "was going to blame me for Joan's return." When Joan goes missing, the scene is presented directly after the emergency room visit, as if Esther's bloody experience precipitated Joan's relapse. Joan is discovered the next morning in the woods. She has hanged herself. Symbolically, Joan, as Esther's double, must die in order for Esther to live: "The novel's repeated references to the promise of rebirth seem to be finally realised when Esther survives and is apparently healed by her therapy; the suicide of her double, Joan Gilling, is an integral part of this symbolic pattern" (Kendell 56). But the suicide also serves to reinforce stereotypes of the self-destructive homosexual unable to be a part of society. It also suggests that heterosexuality is the viable path for women who seek stability: "Joan, the woman who loves other women and who, therefore, can pursue a career and an independent life without benefit of men or marriage, must be disposed of if the demons that haunt Plath's/Esther's mind are to be exorcized as well" (Bennett 130). Esther loses her virginity to a man and is on her way to recovery, while Joan, the lesbian, takes her own life. "In killing off Joan, Plath cancels for Esther the possibility of tenderness" (Bonds 59).

In Chapter 20, Esther is about to be discharged from the hospital and return to college. She realizes that people will treat her differently, as she has witnessed in the way her mother acts toward her, making her feel guilty for her sickness: "A daughter in an asylum! I had done that to her. Still, she had obviously decided to forgive me." Her mother thinks that they both should look back on this "as if all this were a bad dream." Esther is now more confident, more forgiving, and more willing to face her emotions as she moves toward recovery, but still she fears her illness: "To the person in the bell jar, blank and stopped as a dead baby, the world itself is the bad dream." Though her mother encourages her to forget, Esther "remembered everything." Everything she experienced and the people she encountered remain "a part of me. They were my landscape." Furthermore, any facile distinction between "normal" and "abnormal" becomes blurred and more difficult to easily discern, as Esther observes: "What was there about us, in Belsize, so different from the girls playing bridge and gossiping and studying in the college to which I would return? Those girls, too, sat under bell jars of a sort." Esther will leave the hospital with a more sophisticated understanding of the world and its pressures on women.

Buddy Willard returns to visit her, and she feels "nothing but a great, amiable boredom." He seems less confident and is worried that he dated both her and Joan: "Do you think there's something in me that *drives* women crazy?" In response, Esther "burst out laughing," the first time she has laughed since the beginning of the novel. She now seems much more experienced and wiser than Buddy, assuring him, "You had nothing to do with us, Buddy." Buddy wonders who would marry Esther, given her history of mental instability, and his concerns echo her own anxieties on the subject: "I didn't know who would marry me now that I'd been where I had been." Such considerations do not seem to upset her, though, as they would have before her progress at the hospital. Esther symbolically separates herself from the men who have hurt her by calling Irwin to demand that he pay the hospital bill. She makes it clear she does not want to see him again, and in asserting so, she realizes, "I was perfectly free."

At the end of the novel, Esther, considered by Joan's parents to be "one of Joan's best friends," attends the funeral. After Joan's suicide, Esther asked Dr. Nolan if she was responsible for Joan's death—perhaps grappling with feelings of guilt for the way she treated Joan. Dr. Nolan, angry for the first time, tells her that Joan did this to herself. At the funeral, Esther listens to her heart beat its mantra, I am, I am, I am, but this time, the beating of her heart is hopeful, a reminder of life. She no longer wants to die and views Joan's suicide as a waste of a life. She looks at Joan's body and "wondered what I thought I was burying." The burial of Joan symbolizes Esther's burial of the illness and her old imprisoned self.

In the final scene, Esther is about to be interviewed by the doctors, after which she will be free to leave. She is nervous at the prospect of walking out the doors and into her future. Most critics feel the ending is positive. However, Diane S. Bonds questions whether Esther's identity is really now whole and unfragmented or if the ending "leaves Esther prey to defining herself unwittingly and unwillingly in relation to all that remains to her: culturally-ingrained stereotypes of women" (50). Critic Tim Kendall also asserts that the opening and the ending of the novel undercut any possibility of full recovery:

> In fact, *The Bell Jar* provides no definitive means of judging the success of Esther's treatment. The effect is profoundly unsettling. Giving herself the benefit of hindsight, Esther sounds like an omniscient narrator, until it becomes clear that she remains implicated in the breakdown of her younger self, and is still not free: she reveals a fear in the final pages that her recovery may only have been temporary (58).

It is true that the illness may return, but for now, Esther emerges from the experience a more confident woman. Unlike the lobotomized Valerie, she does not want to stay in the hospital. She is ready to face life, even with the risks: "How did I know that someday—at college, in Europe, somewhere, anywhere—the bell jar, with its stifling distortions, wouldn't descend again?" Though the image of the bell jar, with its associations of suffocation and illness, may return, the ending is hopeful, signifying Esther's recovery, independence, and reclaiming of her identity. She considers the release from the hospital to be a rebirth but also recognizes her vulnerability; she is not brand new but "patched, retreaded and approved for the road."

## HOWARD MOSS ON ILLNESS AND DISCLOSURE IN THE NOVEL

The story of a poet who tries to end her life written by a poet who did, Sylvia Plath's *The Bell Jar* was first published under a pseudonym in England in 1963, one month before she committed suicide. We had to wait almost a decade for its publication in the United States, but it was reissued in England in 1966 under its author's real name. A biographical note in the present edition makes it plain that the events in the novel closely parallel Sylvia Plath's twentieth year. For reasons for which we are not wholly to blame, our approach to the novel is impure; *The Bell Jar* is fiction that cannot escape being read in part as autobiography. It begins in New York with an ominous lightness, grows darker as it moves to Massachusetts, then slips slowly into madness. Esther Greenwood, one of a dozen girls in and on the town for a month as "guest editors" of a teenage fashion magazine, is the product of a German immigrant family and a New England suburb. With "fifteen years of straight A's" behind her, a depressing attachment to a dreary but handsome medical student, Buddy Willard, still unresolved, and a yearning to be a poet, she is the kind of girl who doesn't know what drink to order or how much to tip a taxi driver but is doing her thesis on the "twin images" in *Finnegans Wake*, a book she has never managed to finish. Her imagination is at war with the small-town tenets of New England and the big-time sham of New York. She finds it impossible to be one of the army of college girls whose education is a forced stop on the short march to marriage. The crises of identity, sexuality, and survival are grim, and often funny. Wit, irony, and intelligence, as well as an inexplicable, withdrawn sadness, separate Esther from her companions. Being an involuntary truth-seeker, she uses irony as a weapon of judgment, and she is its chief victim. Unable to experience or mime emotions, she feels defective as a person.

The gap between her and the world widens: "I couldn't get myself to react. I felt very still and very empty...." "The silence depressed me. It wasn't the silence of silence. It was my own silence...." "That morning I had tried to hang myself."

Camouflage and illness go together in *The Bell Jar*; moreover, illness is often used to lift or tear down a façade. Doreen, a golden girl of certainty admired by Esther, begins the process by getting drunk. The glimpse of her lying with her head in a pool of her own vomit in a hotel hallway is repellant but crucial. Her illness is followed by a mass ptomaine poisoning at a "fashion" lunch. Buddy gets tuberculosis and goes off to a sanatorium. Esther, visiting him, breaks her leg skiing. When she has her first sexual experience, with a young math professor she has picked up, she hemorrhages.

Taken in by a lesbian friend, she winds up in a hospital. Later, she learns that the friend has hanged herself. A plain recital of the events in *The Bell Jar* would be ludicrous if they were not balanced by genuine desperation at one side of the scale and a sure sense of black comedy at the other. Sickness and disclosure are the keys to *The Bell Jar*. On her last night in New York, Esther climbs to the roof of her hotel and throws her city wardrobe over the parapet, piece by piece. By the end of the novel, she has tried to get rid of her very life, which is given back to her by another process of divestment—psychiatry. Pain and gore are endemic to *The Bell Jar*, and they are described objectively, self-mockingly, almost humorously to begin with. Taken in by the tone (the first third of *The Bell Jar* might be a mordant, sick-joke version of *Breakfast at Tiffany's*), the reader is being lured into the lion's den—that sterile cement room in the basement of a mental hospital where the electric-shock-therapy machine waits for its frightened clients.

The casualness with which physical suffering is treated suggests that Esther is cut off from the instinct for sympathy right from the beginning—for herself as well as for others. Though she is enormously aware of the impingements of sensation, her sensations remain impingements. She lives close to the nerve, but the nerve has become detached from the general network. A thin layer of glass separates her from everyone, and the novel's title, itself made of glass, is evolved from her notion of disconnection: the head of each mentally ill person is enclosed in a bell jar, choking on its own foul air.

Torn between conflicting roles—the sweetheart-*Hausfrau*-mother and "the life of the poet," neither very real to her—Esther finds life itself inimical. Afraid of distorting the person she is yet to become, she becomes the ultimate distortion—nothing. As she descends into the pit of depression, the world is a series of wrong reverberations: her mother's face is a perpetual accusation; the wheeling of a baby carriage underneath her window, a grinding irritation. She becomes obsessed by the idea of suicide, and one of the great achievements of *The Bell Jar* is that it makes real the subtle distinctions between a distorted viewpoint and the distortions inherent in what it sees. Convention may contribute to Esther's insanity, but she never loses her awareness of the irrationality of convention. Moved to Belsize, a part of the mental hospital reserved for patients about to go back to the world, she makes the connection explicit:

> What was there about us, in Belsize, so different from the girls playing bridge and gossiping and studying in the college to which I would return? Those girls, too, sat under bell jars of a sort.

Terms like "mad" and "sane" grow increasingly inadequate as the action develops. Esther is "psychotic" by definition, but the definition is merely a descriptive tag: by the time we learn how she got to be "psychotic" the word has ceased to be relevant. (As a work of fiction, *The Bell Jar* seems to complement the clinical theories of the Scottish analyst R. D. Laing.) Because it is written from the distraught observer's point of view rather than from the viewpoint of someone observing her, there is continuity to her madness; it is not one state suddenly supplanting another but the most gradual of processes.

Suicide, a grimly compulsive game of fear and guilt, as addictive as alcohol or drugs, is experimental at first—a little blood here, a bit of choking there, just to see what it will be like. It quickly grows into an overwhelming desire for annihilation. By the time Esther climbs into the crawl space of a cellar and swallows a bottle of sleeping pills—by the time we are faced by the real thing—the event, instead of seeming grotesque, seems like a natural consequence. When she is about to leave the hospital, after a long series of treatments, her psychiatrist tells her to consider her breakdown "a bad dream." Esther, "patched, retreaded, and approved for the road," thinks, "To the person in the bell jar, blank and stopped as a dead baby, the world itself is the bad dream."

That baby is only one of many in *The Bell Jar*. They smile up from the pages of magazines, they sit like little freaks pickled in glass jars on display in the pediatric ward of Buddy's hospital. A "sweet baby cradled in its mother's belly" seems to wait for Esther at the end of the ski run when she has her accident. And in the course of the novel she witnesses a birth. In place of her never-to-be-finished thesis on the "twin images" in *Finnegans Wake*, one might be written on the number and kinds of babies that crop up in *The Bell Jar*. In a gynecologist's office, watching a mother fondling her baby, Esther wonders why she is so separated from this easy happiness, this carrying out of the prescribed biological and social roles. She does not want a baby; she is a baby herself. But she is also a potential writer. She wants to fulfill herself, not to *be* fulfilled. To her, babies are The Trap, and sex is the bait. But she is too intelligent not to realize that babies don't represent life—they *are* life, though not necessarily the kind Esther wants to live; that is, if she wants to live at all. She is caught between the monstrous fetuses on display in Buddy's ward and the monstrous slavery of the seemingly permanent pregnancy of her neighbor Dodo Conway, who constantly wheels a baby carriage under Esther's window, like a demented figure in a Greek chorus. Babies lure Esther toward suicide by luring her toward a life she cannot—literally—bear. There seem to be only two solutions, and both involve the invisible: to pledge faith to the unborn or fealty to the dead. Life, so painfully visible and present, defeats her, and she takes it, finally, into her own hands. With the exception of the psychiatrist's disinterested affection for her, love is either missing or unrecognized in *The Bell Jar*. Its overwhelming emotion is disgust—disgust that has not yet become contempt and is therefore more damaging.

## VANCE BOURJAILY ON PSEUDONYMS AND ALTERNATE IDENTITIES

In New York, Esther is especially attracted by two of the other winners, both blondes—a decadent, flamboyant platinum number called Doreen, and a sweet, wholesome daisy of a girl named Betsy. Esther can't decide which she'd rather be like. When she attaches herself to Doreen, they are picked up by a disc jockey named Lenny, with eyes for Doreen. Esther invents for herself a drab, protective identity as Elly Higginbottom. When Esther/Elly leaves the pair in Lenny's apartment, to walk back alone to her hotel through the New York night, Doreen and Lenny have been jitterbugging, kissing, and biting, and Doreen is being whirled on the disc jockey's shoulder, belly-down and breasts out.

Late that night, Esther is waked up by Doreen's voice at her door saying "Elly, Elly, Elly," while a hotel maid calls "'Miss Greenwood, Miss Greenwood, Miss Greenwood,' as if I had a split personality or something" (p. 17). Opening the door, she finds Doreen slumped against the jamb, drunk and grown dark and heavy. Doreen collapses in her own vomit at Esther's door.

When Esther attaches herself to Betsy, they do what is expected of them. They behave with girlish propriety—though Esther is covertly gobbling Betsy's caviar—at an elaborate luncheon. This, too, ends in vomit as the whole crew of nice young editors is struck down by ptomaine. Doreen has stayed away.

Recovering, Esther detaches herself, and operates next on her own. She offers her burdensome virginity, one evening, to a United Nations simultaneous interpreter named Constantin. Though they lie down together, he will do no

63

more than squeeze her hand, touch her hair, and go to sleep. Consequently, she fails to catch up in sexual experience with Buddy Willard, the Yale medical student whom it was assumed Esther would marry. Buddy's courtship, told in interspersed flashbacks, has been agreeably gruesome, featuring her attendance at the dissection of cadavers; a tour of the exhibit of pickled, premature babies; a lecture during which sickle-cell anemia victims were wheeled onto the platform; and a bloody childbirth. There was also a ski trip during which Esther broke her leg, an evening when Buddy exhibited himself—and the boy is now tubercular. But Esther's reason for rejecting him, as she does, is Buddy's confessional boasting of a consummated summer affair with a waitress.

At the opening of the book, and recurring as a prelude to Esther's final New York indignity, are passages about the real horror she feels at the impending electrocution of Julius and Ethel Rosenberg. When the indignity occurs, Esther is Doreen's satellite once more. Doreen has arranged a date for her reticent friend.

"'Honestly,'" Doreen promises, "'This one'll be different'" (p. 84). He sure is.

Marco is an immaculate Peruvian who tangos masterfully with Esther, escorts her outdoors, knocks her down in the mud and tries to rape her. When she bloodies his nose, he marks her cheeks with his blood.

The first part, and the New York adventure, end with Esther on the hotel roof, just before dawn, throwing out into the darkness, item by item, the expensive, not-quite-sophisticated wardrobe bought with scholarship money for the trip.

She goes home by train to Route 28, outside of Boston, wearing a silly dirndl skirt and frilled white blouse. Marco's blood is still on Esther's face.

Though the tone of much of this is wry, reminiscently detached, even amusing, it shows us Esther on her way down into melancholia, with little spurts toward recovery after each of which the psychotic despair deepens. There is evidence enough to justify using some harsh, psychiatrist's jargon about her—words like narcissistic and infantile—but if each quality is there, it is so only in such measure as seems normal for a vulnerable, imaginative, mostly appealing young woman, at odds with society. What is not normal is the growing split we are shown into the two selves, Esther and the very-much lesser, unappealing self she has named Elly Higginbottom.

In the second part of *The Bell Jar*, returned to a depressing Boston suburban home with her widowed mother, Esther is neither a Doreen nor a Betsy, but only Elly now. And while poor, dull Elly tells a young sailor, whom she allows to pick her up on the Boston Common, that she comes from Chicago, her real home is underneath a bell jar, an archaic laboratory fixture for displaying specimens. The specimen, on its dark base, is kept airtight, dust-free and out of contact, by a cylindrical glass cover. We can see it well enough, but if we imagine the specimen itself having life inside, the sights and sounds which reach it through the suffocating glass are distorted, muffled, and meaningless.

Our specimen, Elly Higginbottom, doesn't want to be alive. In this second part of the book, she tries, with razor blades, by drowning, and by hanging, to kill herself. At last, using sleeping pills, she so nearly succeeds that the search for and discovery of her drugged body are the subject of tabloid news stories.

During this section she has been seen by a disastrously unprofessional psychiatrist named Gordon with "eyelashes so long and thick they looked almost artificial" and features "so perfect he was almost pretty" (p. 105). When she has finished telling him that she cannot sleep or eat or read, Dr. Gordon asks (p. 107):

> "Where did you say you went to college?"
> Baffled, I told him. I didn't see where college fitted in.
> "Ah!" Dr. Gordon leaned back in his chair, staring . . . over my shoulder with a reminiscent smile. . . .
> "I remember your college well. I was up there during the war. They had a WAC station, didn't they? Or was it WAVES? . . . Yes, a WAC station. I remember now . . . my, they were a pretty bunch of girls."
> Dr. Gordon laughed.

He decides to try electroshock therapy, and bungles it. The sleeping pills are only a few days off, now, for Esther/Elly. She takes fifty of them.

In part three, institutionalized, given increasingly better psychiatric care, and finally successful shock treatments, Elly sees the cover of the bell jar start to rise, and begins to emerge as Esther once again.

In the hospital with her is someone she knew at college named Joan Gilling. Joan has also been a near-fiancée to Buddy Willard, and also a campus achiever. Joan, reading in the papers of Esther/Elly's suicide attempt, a few weeks back, was actually led to emulate it, going off to New York to try to kill herself.

As Esther improves, Joan declines. Near the end of the book, Esther, on parole, finally manages to get rid of her virginity in a painful, rather impersonal way, and is satisfied with herself if not by the instrumental stranger she has chosen, whom she only sees once. Joan's new experience is homosexual, with another inmate. As Esther is ready to face the committee of doctors who will release her to return to college, news comes that Joan has slipped away in the night, to the woods, by the frozen ponds, has hanged herself and is dead.

## ROBERT SCHOLES ON PLATH'S USE OF REALISM

*The Bell Jar* is about the way this country was in the Fifties and about the way it is to lose one's grip on sanity and recover it again. It is easy to say (and it is said too often) that insanity is the only sane reaction to the America of recent years. And it is also said frequently (especially by R. D. Laing and his followers) that the only thing to do about madness is relax and enjoy it. But neither of these "clever" responses to her situation occur to Esther Greenwood, who is the narrator and central character in *The Bell Jar*.

To Esther, madness is the descent of a stifling bell jar over her head. In this state, she says, "wherever I sat . . . I would be sitting under the same glass bell jar, stewing in my sour air." And she adds, "To the person in the bell jar, blank and stopped as a dead baby, the world itself is the bad dream." Which is not to say that Esther believes the world outside the asylum is full of people living an authentic existence. She asks, "What was there about us, in Belsize, so different from the girls playing bridge and gossiping and studying in the college to which I would return? Those girls, too, sat under bell jars of a sort."

The world in which the events of this novel take place is a world bounded by the cold war on one side and the sexual war on the other. We follow Esther Greenwood's personal life from her summer job in New York with *Ladies' Day* magazine, back through her days at New England's largest school for women, and forward through her attempted suicide, her bad treatment at one asylum and her good treatment at another, to her final reentry into the world like a used tire: "patched, retreaded, and approved for the road."

But this personal life is delicately related to larger events—especially the execution of the Rosenbergs, whose impending death by electrocution is introduced in the stunning first paragraph of the book. Ironically, that same electrical power which destroys the Rosenbergs restores Esther to life. It is shock therapy which finally lifts the bell jar and enables Esther to breathe freely once again. Passing through death she is reborn. This novel is not political or historical in any narrow sense; but in looking at the madness of the world and the world of madness, it forces us to consider the great questions posed by all truly realistic fiction: what is reality and how can it be confronted?

In *The Bell Jar*, Sylvia Plath has used superbly the most important technical device of realism—what the Russian critic Viktor Shklovsky called "defamiliarization." True realism defamiliarizes our world so that it emerges from the dust of habitual acceptance and becomes visible once again. This is quite the opposite of that comforting false realism that presents the world in terms of clichés that we are all too ready to accept.

Sylvia Plath's technique of defamiliarization ranges from tiny verbal witticisms that bite, to images that are deeply troubling. When she calls the hotel for women that Esther inhabits in New York the "Amazon," she is not merely enjoying the closeness of the sound of that word to "Barbizon," she is forcing us to rethink the entire concept of a hotel for women: "mostly girls of my age with wealthy parents who wanted to be sure that their daughters would be living where men couldn't get at them and deceive them." And she is announcing a major theme in her work, the hostility between men and women.

With Esther Greenwood this hostility takes the form of obsessive attempts to get herself liberated from a virginity she finds oppressive, by a masculinity she finds hideous. When her medical student boyfriend suggests that they play a round of the traditional children's game—I'll show you mine if you show me yours—she looks at his naked maleness and reacts this way: "The only thing I could think of was turkey neck and turkey gizzards and I felt very depressed." This is defamiliarization with a vengeance. The image catches up all cocky masculine pride of flesh and reduces it to the level of giblets. It sees the inexorable link between generation and death and makes us see it too, because the image is so fitting. All flesh comes from this—and comes to this.

In the face of such cosmic disgust, psychological explanations like "penis envy" seem pitifully inadequate. Esther Greenwood is not a woman who wants to be a man but a human being who cannot avoid seeing that the price we pay for life is death. Sexual differentiation itself is only a metaphor for human incompletion. The battle of the sexes is, after all, a civil war.

Esther Greenwood's account of her year in the bell jar is as clear and readable as it is witty and disturbing. It makes for a novel such as Dorothy Parker might have written if she had not belonged to a generation infected with the relentless frivolity of the college-humor magazine. The brittle humor of that earlier generation is reincarnated in *The Bell Jar*, but raised to a more serious level because it is recognized as a resource of hysteria.

68

One of the most misunderstood of contemporary novels, Sylvia Plath's *The Bell Jar* is in structure and intent a highly conventional *bildungsroman*. Concerned almost entirely with the education and maturation of Esther Greenwood, Plath's novel uses a chronological and necessarily episodic structure to keep Esther at the center of all action. Other characters are fragmentary, subordinate to Esther and her developing consciousness, and are shown only through their effects on her as central character. No incident is included which does not influence her maturation, and the most important formative incidents occur in the city, New York. As Jerome Buckley describes the *bildungsroman* in his 1974 *Season of Youth*, its principal elements are "a growing up and gradual self-discovery," "alienation," "provinciality, the larger society," "the conflict of generations," "ordeal by love" and "the search for a vocation and a working philosophy."[1]

Plath signals the important change of location at the opening of *The Bell Jar*. "It was it a queer, sultry summer, the summer they electrocuted the Rosenbergs, and I didn't know what I was doing in New York. . . . New York was bad enough. By nine in the morning the fake, country-wet freshness that somehow seeped in overnight evaporated like the tail end of a sweet dream. Mirage-gray at the bottom of their granite canyons, the hot streets wavered in the sun, the car tops sizzled and glittered, and the dry, cindery dust blew into my eyes and down my throat."[2] Displaced, misled by the morning freshness, Greenwood describes a sterile, inimical setting for her descent into, and exploration of, a hell both personal and communal. Readers have often stressed the analogy between Greenwood and the Rosenbergs—and sometimes lamented the inappropriateness of Plath's comparing her personal angst with their actual execution[3]—but in this opening description, the Rosenberg execution is just one of the threatening elements present in the New York context. It is symptomatic of the "foreign" country's hostility, shown in a myriad of ways throughout the novel.

In *The Bell Jar*, as in the traditional *bildungsroman*, the character's escape to a city images the opportunity to find self as well as truths about life. Such characters as Pip, Paul Morel, and Jude Fawley idealize the city as a center of learning and experience, and think that once they have relocated themselves, their lives will change dramatically. As Buckley points out, however, the city is often ambivalent: "the city, which seems to promise infinite variety and newness, all too often brings a disenchantment more alarming and decisive than any dissatisfaction with the narrowness of provincial life."[4] For Esther Greenwood, quiet Smith student almost delirious with the opportunity to go to New York and work for *Ladies' Day* for a month, the disappointment of her New York experience is cataclysmic. Rather than shape her life, it nearly ends it; and Plath structures the novel to show the process of disenchantment in rapid acceleration.

The novel opens in the midst of Greenwood's month in New York, although she tells the story in flashbacks; and for the first half of the book—ten of its twenty chapters—attention remains there, or on past experiences that are germane to the New York experiences. Greenwood recounts living with the other eleven girls on the *Ladies' Day* board at the Amazon Hotel, doing assignments for the tough fiction editor Jay Cee, going to lunches and dances, buying clothes, dating men very unlike the fellows she had known at college, and sorting through lifestyles like Doreen's which shock, bewilder, and yet fascinate her. Events as predictably mundane as these are hardly the stuff of exciting fiction but Plath has given them an unexpected drama because of the order in which they appear. *The Bell Jar* is plotted to establish two primary themes: that of Greenwood's developing identity, or lack of it; and that of her battle against submission to the authority of both older people and, more pertinently, of men. The second theme is sometimes absorbed by the first but Plath uses enough imagery of sexual conquest that it comes to have an almost equal importance. For a woman of the 1950s, finding an identity other than that of sweetheart, girlfriend, and wife and mother was a major achievement.

Greenwood's search for identity is described through a series of episodes that involve possible role models. Doreen, the Southern woman whose rebelliousness fascinates Esther, knows exactly what she will do with her time in New York. The first scene in the novel is Doreen's finding the macho Lenny Shepherd, disc jockey and playboy par excellence. Attracted by Doreen's "decadence," Esther goes along with the pair until the sexual jitterbug scene ends with Doreen's melon-like breasts flying out of her dress after she has bitten Lenny's ear lobe. Esther has called herself *Elly Higginbottom* in this scene, knowing instinctively that she wants to be protected from the kind of knowledge Doreen has. Plath describes Esther as a photo negative, a small black dot, a hole in the ground, and when she walks the 48 blocks home to the Amazon in panic, she sees no one recognizable in the mirror. Some Chinese woman, she thinks, "wrinkled and used up," and, later, "the reflection in a ball of dentist's mercury" (20–1). Purging herself in a hot bath, Greenwood temporarily escapes her own consciousness: "Doreen is dissolving, Lenny Shepherd is dissolving, Frankie is dissolving, New York is dissolving, they are all dissolving away and none of them matter any more. I don't know them. I have never known them and I am very pure" (22). Unfortunately, when Doreen pounds on her door later that night, drunk and sick, Esther has to return to the real world. Her revulsion is imaged in Doreen's uncontrollable vomit.

The second "story" of the New York experience is the ptomaine poisoning of all the girls except Doreen after the *Ladies' Day* magazine luncheon. Plath's vignette of Jay Cee is imbedded in this account; the editor's great disappointment in Greenwood (because she has no motivation, no direction) serves to make Esther more depressed. As she comes near death from the poisoning, she also assesses the female role models available to her: her own mother, who urges her to learn shorthand; the older writer Philomena Guinea, who has befriended her but prescriptively; and Jay Cee, by now an admonitory figure. Although Esther feels "purged and holy and ready for a new life after her ordeal (52), she cannot rid herself of the feeling of betrayal. No sooner had she realized Jay Cee ("I wished I had a mother like Jay Cee. Then I'd know what to do") than she had disappointed her. The development of the novel itself illustrates the kind of irony Esther had employed in the preface, with the lament

> I was supposed to be having the time of my life.
> I was supposed to be the envy of thousands of other college girls just like me all over America. . . .
> Look what can happen in this country, they'd say. A girl lives in some out-of-the-way town for nineteen years, so poor she can't afford a magazine, and then she gets a scholarship to college and wins a prize here and a prize there and ends up steering New York like her own private car.
> Only I wasn't steering anything, not even myself (2–3).

Plath's handling of these early episodes makes clear Greenwood's very real confusion about her direction. As Buckley has pointed out, the apparent conflict with parent or location in the *bildungsroman* is secondary to the real conflict, which remains "personal in origin; the problem lies with the hero himself"[5] (or herself).

Esther Greenwood's struggle to know herself, to be self-motivated, to become a writer as she has always dreamed is effectively presented through Plath's comparatively fragmented structure. As Patricia Meyer Spacks writes in 1981 about literature of the adolescent, the adolescent character has no self to discover. The process is not one of discovering a persona already there but rather creating a persona.[6] Unlike Esther, then, perhaps we should not be disturbed that the face in her mirror is mutable. We must recognize with sympathy, however, that she carries the weight of having to maintain a number of often conflicting identities—the obliging daughter and the ungrateful woman, the successful writer and the immature student, the virginal girlfriend and the worldly lover. In its structure *The Bell Jar* shows how closely these strands are interwoven.

While Plath is ostensibly writing about Esther's New York experiences and her quest for a female model, she regularly interjects comments about Buddy Willard, the Yale medical student who has proposed to Esther. Early references to him connect him with the haunting childbirth scene and the bottled foetuses and cadavers he has introduced Esther to. That these images are all connected with women's traditional choices in life—to become mothers—begins to frame the essential conflict between Buddy and Esther. From chapters five through eight Plath describes the romance between the two, but the extensive flashback seems less an intrusion than an explication. Esther is what she is in New York because of the indoctrination she has had at the hands of her socially-approved guide, Buddy Willard. For Buddy, women are helpmeets, submissive to husband's wishes; they have no identity in themself. Esther's desire to become a poet is nonsense (poems are "dust" in his vocabulary); her true role is to be virginal and accepting of his direction—whether the terrain be sex or skiing. More explicit than their conversations are the images Plath chooses to describe Esther during this section, images of frustration and futility.

One central image is that of the fig tree, first introduced after Esther has nearly died from food poisoning and is reading the stories *Ladies' Day* has sent the convalescents. Lush in its green spring, the fig tree nourishes the love of an unaware couple. In contrast, Esther describes her love for Buddy as dying,

> we had met together under our own imaginary fig tree, and what we had seen wasn't a bird coming out of an egg but a baby coming out of a woman, and then something awful happened and we went our separate ways (61).

When the fig tree metaphor recurs to Esther, she sees it filled with fat purple figs ("one fig was a husband and a happy home and children, and another fig was a famous poet and another fig was a brilliant professor, and another fig was Ee Gee, the amazing editor. . . ." 84–5). She sits in the crotch of the tree, however, "starving to death, just because I couldn't make up my mind which of the figs I would choose. I wanted each and every one of them, but choosing one meant losing all the rest." The dilemma of her adolescence—unlike that of most men—was that any choice was also a relinquishing. Greenwood believed firmly that there was no way, in the American culture of the 1950s, that a talented woman could successfully combine a professional career with homemaking. As Mrs. Willard kept insisting, "What a man is is an arrow into the future and what a woman is is the place the arrow shoots off from" (79).

Eventually, in Esther's metaphor, the figs rot and die, a conclusion which aligns the image tonally with the rest of the novel. In her highly visual presentation of Esther's education, Plath consistently shows characters who are poisoned, diseased, injured, bloodied, and even killed. The violence of her characterization seems a fitting parallel for the intensity of her feelings about the dilemmas Greenwood faces as she matures. (Again, in Spacks' words, "The great power implicitly assigned to adolescents in social science studies belongs to them only as a group. As individuals, psychological commentary makes clear, they suffer uncertainty, absence of power."[7]) Greenwood's persona is clearly marked by feelings of "uncertainty," based on her all-too-sharp understanding of her "absence of power." When Buddy, who has never skied himself, "instructs" her in the sport and encourages her in the long run that breaks her leg in two places, she obeys him almost mindlessly. (The fact that she finds a sense of self and power in the run is an unexpected benefit for her.) Buddy's malevolence as he diagnoses the breaks and predicts that she will be in a cast for months is a gleeful insight into his real motives for maintaining their relationship while he is hospitalized for tuberculosis. Esther is his possession, his security, his way of keeping his own self image normal in the midst of his increasing plumpness and his fear of disease.

Buddy's sadistic treatment of Esther prepares the way for the last New York episode, Esther's date with the cruel woman-hater, Marco. Replete with scenes of violence, sexual aggression, mud and possession, this last of the New York stories plunges the reader further into the relentless depravity the city has provided. Marco's brutal rape attempt and his marking Esther with blood from his bleeding nose are physically even more insulting than his calling her *slut*. But even though the men in Esther's life are responsible for these events, Plath shows clearly that Esther's passivity and her lack of questioning are also responsible. Esther's malaise has made her incapable of dealing with aggression either subtle or overt—except privately. Once she has returned to the Amazon, she carries all her expensive clothes to the roof of the hotel and throws them into the sky. Her anger at New York is at least partly misplaced, but Plath has shown that the city and its occupants have exacerbated wounds already given in more provincial and seemingly protective locations. Throwing out her clothes is tantamount to rejecting the traditional image of pretty, smart girl, object for man's acquisition (the use throughout the novel of the *Mademoiselle* photographs of the fashionably dressed coeds also builds to this scene).

Unfortunately, once Plath returns home—dressed in Betsy's skirt and blouse and still carrying Marco's blood streaks on her face—she finds that she has been rejected from the prestigious Harvard writing course. That blow destroys the last shred of self image (Greenwood as writer), and the second half of the novel shows Esther's education not in the process of becoming adult but rather in the process of becoming mad. Again, Plath structures the book so that role model figures are introduced and either discredited or approved. Esther's mother, who appears to think her daughter's insanity is just malingering, is quickly discredited. The irony is that Esther not only must live with the woman, she must also share a bedroom (and by implication, the most intimate parts of her life) with her. Joan Gilling, a Smith student and previous rival for Buddy's affections, presents the option of lesbian life, but her own stability has been irrevocably damaged and she later hangs herself. Doctor Norton, Esther's psychiatrist, is the warm, tolerant and just mentor whose efforts to help Esther understand herself are quickly rewarded. Doctor Norton gives her leave to both hate her mother, and the attitudes she represents, and to be fitted with a diaphragm, so that the previously closed world of sexual experience will be open to her. As Plath has presented both areas of experience throughout the novel, Esther needs to be free from conventional judgments so that she will not absorb so much guilt. One of the most telling scenes in the second half of the book is her reaction to her first electroshock treatment. "I wondered what terrible thing it was that I had done" (161).

The relentless guilt Esther feels as she looks from her bedroom window and sees the neighbor Dodo Conway, wheeling her latest child of six while she is pregnant with the seventh, brings all the scattered images of childbirth and female responsibility to a climax. Unless she accepts this role, Esther will have no life—this is the message her society, even the most supportive elements in it, gives her. But Plath has used one key image during the childbirth scene, that of a "long, blind, doorless and windowless corridor of pain . . . waiting to open up and shut her in again" (72), and that image of relentless suffering recurs throughout the second half of *The Bell Jar*. It is, in fact, the title image, an encasement, unrelieved, where Esther is "stewing in my own sour air" (209). More frightening than the bewildering crotch of the fig tree, the bell jar presents no choices, no alternatives, except death. Another late image is that of "a black, airless sack with no way out" (144). Choice has been subsumed to guilty depression, and one of the refrains that haunts Esther is *You'll never get anywhere like that, you'll never get anywhere like that* (164).

And so the second half of the novel becomes a chronicle of Esther's education in suicide and her various suicide attempts. So expertly and completely have the contradictions of her adolescent education been presented in the first ten chapters that Plath needs do very little with background during the second half. Buddy Willard makes only one appearance, wondering sadly who will marry Esther now that she has been "here." Such a scene only confirms the intent of his characterization earlier in the book. Even during the second half of the novel, Esther remains the good student. In her study of suicide, she reads, asks questions, correlates material, chooses according to her own personality, and progresses just as if she were writing a term paper. All factual information is given in the context of *her* needs, however, so the essential charting of Esther's psyche dominates the rest of the book.

Many of the episodes in the latter part of the novel are skeletal. It is as if Plath were loathe to give up any important details but that she also realized that her readers were, in effect, reading two stories. The first half of *The Bell Jar* gives the classic female orientation and education, with obvious indications of the failure of that education appearing near the end of the New York experience. The second half gives an equally classic picture of mental deterioration and its treatment, a picture relatively new to fiction in the late 1950s, important both culturally and personally to Plath. But the exigencies of the fictional form were pressing, and Plath had already crowded many characters and episodes into her structure. The somewhat ambivalent ending may have occurred as much because the book was growing so long as because Plath was uncertain about the outcome of her protagonist. As the text makes clear, the main reason for a fairly open ending is that Esther herself had to remain unsure about the condition of her recovery, about her health in the future: she saw question marks; she hoped the bell jar would not close down again; but she also affirmed that her leaving the asylum was a birth, and that there should be "a ritual for being born twice" (275). The recurrence of the "old brag" of her heart—"I am, I am, I am"—is much more comforting than another time the refrain had occurred, as she contemplated death through drowning.

The Esther Greenwood pictured in the later pages of *The Bell Jar* is a much more confident person.[8] She knows she does not want to be like the lobotomized Valerie, incapable of any emotion. She knows real grief at Joan's funeral, and real anger at Buddy's visit. She understands the enormity of her mother's refusal to accept the truth about her illness, and the corresponding and somewhat compensatory generosity of Doctor Nolan's acceptance of it. Esther is also much more aggressive in her language. For the first time in the years depicted, she speaks directly. "'I have a bill here, Irwin,'" she says quietly to the man who was her first lover. "'I hate her,'" she admits to Doctor Nolan about her mother. "'You had nothing to do with us, Buddy,'" she says scathingly to her former boyfriend. Even early in her breakdown she is quite direct ("I can't sleep. I can't read. . . .") but the irony in these encounters is that no one she speaks with will attend to what she is saying. Various doctors, her mother, friends persist in translating what she is saying ("I haven't slept for fourteen nights") into meanings that are acceptable to them. One climactic scene between Esther and her mother shows this tendency to mishear and misinterpret, and also gives the best description of the bell jar stifling:

> My mother's face floated to mind, a pale, reproachful moon. . . .
> A daughter in an asylum! I had done that to her. Still, she had obviously decided to forgive me.
> "We'll take up where we left off, Esther," she had said, with her sweet, martyr's smile. "We'll act as if all this were a bad dream."
> A bad dream.
> To the person in the bell jar, blank and stopped as a dead baby, the world itself is the bad dream.
> A bad dream.
> I remembered everything.
> I remembered the cadavers and Doreen and the story of the fig tree and Marco's diamond. . . .
> Maybe forgetfulness, like a kind snow, should numb and cover them.
> But they were part of me. They were my landscape (267).

If a woman's life must be suffused with the image of herself as nurturer, mother, passive sustainer, then the most horrible of all negative images is that of a dead baby. Plath's choice of the adjectives *blank* and *stopped* is powerful; these words are unexpected opposites for the clichés usually associated with a child's growth. By implication, Esther places herself in the dual role of child and mother, and finds no satisfaction in either. And in this scene, she finds particularly hateful the fact that her tortuous experience of madness, which has brought her finally to a new stage of development, be written off by her mother as illusory, a bad dream. It is not surprising that she throws away the roses her mother has brought for her birthday, discounting that biological event in favor of the second birth, the rebirth, to be accomplished when she leaves the asylum, with Doctor Nolan as her guide. The closing lines of *The Bell Jar* surely draw a birth scene:

> There ought, I thought, to be a ritual for being born twice—patched, retreaded and approved for the road. I was trying to think of an appropriate one when Doctor Nolan appeared from nowhere and touched me on the shoulder.
> "All right, Esther."
> I rose and followed her to the open door.
> Pausing, for a brief breath, on the threshold, I saw the silver-haired doctor who had told me about the rivers and the Pilgrims on my first day, and the pocked, cadaverous face of Miss Huey, and eyes I thought I had recognized over white masks.
> The eyes and the faces all turned themselves toward me, and guiding myself by them, as by a magical thread, I stepped into the room (275).

In contrast to the doorless blankness of tunnels, sacks, and bell jars, this open door and Esther's ability to breathe are surely positive images.

### Notes

1. Jerome Hamilton Buckley, *Season of Youth, The Bildungsroman from Dickens to Golding* (Cambridge, Mass.: Harvard University Press, 1974), viii, 18. And see C. Hugh Holman ("*The Bildungsroman, American Style*" in *Windows on the World, Essays on American Social Fiction*, Knoxville, The University of Tennessee Press, 1979, pp. 168–97) who stresses that the form is particularly important to American writers because of its search and initiation process.

American experience cries for forms that emphasize "the road to self-discovery"; it is often cast in the form of a story told by a first-person retrospective narrator. After completing this essay, I found an interpretation which also uses the notion of bildungsroman, but approaches it from a highly autobiographical perspective. Readers interested in this subject should see Henry I. Schvey, "Sylvia Plath's *The Bell Jar*: Bildungsroman or Case History," *The Dutch Quarterly Review of Anglo-American Letters*, Vol. 8 (1978), pp. 18–37.

2. Sylvia Plath, *The Bell Jar* (New York: Harper & Row, Publishers, 1971), 1. Hereafter cited in text.

3. Among those critics who objected to the comparison with the Rosenberg execution are Denis Donoghue ("You Could Say She Had a Calling for Death," *New York Times Book Review*, November 22, 1981, p. 30), Saul Maloff ("Waiting for the Voice to Crack," *The New Republic*, 164, May 8, 1971, pp. 33–35) and Charles Molesworth ("Again, Sylvia Plath," *Salmagundi*, 37, Spring, 1977, pp. 140–46). This objection fuses with that about her use of Holocaust imagery (in the poems) to represent her personal condition. See also Jane Marcus, "Nostalgia Is Not Enough: Why Elizabeth Hardwick Misreads Ibsen, Plath, and Wolf" in *Bucknell Review, Women, Literature, Criticism*, ed. Harry R. Garvin (Lewisburg, Pa.: Associated University Press, Inc.), 171.

4. Buckley, 20.

5. Ibid.

6. Patricia Meyer Spacks, *The Adolescent Idea, Myths of Youth and the Adult Imagination* (New York: Basic Books, Inc., 1981), 45.

7. Ibid.

8. See Barbara Hill Rigney, *Madness and Sexual Politics in the Feminist Novel* (Madison: University of Wisconsin Press, 1978); Patricia Meyer Spacks, "A Chronicle of Women," *Hudson Review*, 25, Spring, 1972, p. 164; and Howard Moss, "Dying: An Introduction," *New Yorker*, 47, July 10, 1971, pp. 73–75, for complementary interpretations.

# E. MILLER BUDICK ON PLATH'S FEMINIST DISCOURSE

Esther's college, Jay Cee, and *Ladies' Day* all represent female environments that ought to have provided Esther with the language and identity she seeks. But each has abnegated authority, either by allowing male language to infect and dominate female expression or by giving up on expression altogether. Each, therefore, contributes to the ultimately self-annihilating distortion of Esther's basic instincts, rendering them voiceless cries of help.

Jay Cee's culpability is instructive. As a woman, Jay Cee represents the potential for female discourse. Her office is filled with "potted plants, shelf after shelf of them, springing up at her back like a tropical garden" (32). Jay Cee might well speak the botanical language. But Jay Cee abbreviates her identity, her initials substituting for a name. With her "brutal promptitude" and shrunken eclipse of language ("Jay Cee Here"), she speaks a man's language and represents a man's aesthetic (31). Jay Cee represents the path that many women, including women writers, have chosen. Writes Elaine Showalter, in *A Literature of Their Own*, "The feminists' urge to break away from the yoke of biological femininity also expressed itself as a wish to be male" (192). "You'll never get anywhere like that," Jay Cee warns Esther; "What languages do you have?" (34). Esther's response to Jay Cee's question mirrors her earlier college reaction. On the one hand, she pretends to conform to the world's demands: she promises to learn this masculine language of her younger brother and of her dead father, from "some manic-depressive hamlet in the black heart of Prussia." She knows that it is the language for which her mother is "stoned" (34). She recognizes it as a language of death that makes her mind "shut like a clam" (echoing the power of physics to make her mind go dead) and which "barbed-wire"-like threatens to assault her (34; the word "barbed" recalls the phallic threat of the "scorpion" and "mosquito" associated with chemistry and physics). But she promises anyway. On the other hand, she withdraws from her promise (35). Esther's retreat is a running blind. She apes precisely the language she so abhors ("I'll see what I can do. I probably might just fit in one of those double-barrelled, accelerated courses in elementary German they've rigged" [35]). And she descends into the memory of a similarly wounding and self-deceptive escape that, inexplicable to her, provides no redress to her present situation.

Esther looks to Jay Cee as a source of a female language through which she can enter into meaningful discourse with the world. She wishes Jay Cee were her mother and believes that if she were all of her problems would be solved. But Jay Cee is only another version of female submission. She is the masculine in female disguise. She knows "languages," but only to edit them. She is not herself a source of language. It is not surprising that it is impossible for Esther "to imagine Jay Cee out of her strict office suit and luncheon-duty hat and in bed with her fat husband" (6); nor is it odd that Jay Cee should cause Esther to recognize her "real father" (34) or that Esther should see Mr. Manzi emerging from the back of Jay Cee's head, coming out of the "hat" (39) with which both are associated. Like Esther's real mother, the language Jay Cee teaches is a male-oriented shorthand that reduces Esther to the same abbreviated, fragmented sense of self ("Ee Gee" [40]) with which physics and chemistry threaten her. "I hated the idea of serving men in any way," she says. "I wanted to dictate my own thrilling letters. Besides, those little shorthand symbols in the book my mother showed me seemed just as bad as let $t$ equal time and let $s$ equal the total distance" (79). And later: "The only thing was, when I tried to picture myself in some job, briskly jotting down line after line of shorthand my mind went blank . . . as I sat there and watched, the white chalk curlicues blurred into senselessness" (128).

Nor is the world of *Ladies' Day* the source of the language Esther craves. *Ladies' Day* teaches not self-expression but how to serve men—almost literally. Seated at a table emblematic of the cloying excess of female domesticity, Esther gorges herself in a stereotype of worshipful, repressive female hunger (27–28); the grotesqueness of overeating and its relation to female sexuality are picked up in the hospitalization scenes later on and in the consequences of Esther's insulin therapy. Esther's gluttony results not only in a deathlike physical illness anticipating her suicide attempt, but also the total silence in which suicide also culminates. Her lips produce only a parody of botanical richness and fulness—the "fuzzy pink-lip shape [that] bloomed right in the middle of [her] napkin like a tiny heart" (50), that represents the imprint, not of language, but of silence. When they open again, her lips only spew forth the consequences of the poison, contained appropriately enough in the "bland," "pink-mottled claw-meat" (50; Dr. Gordon's language also conceals a "claw" [137]).

Implicit in the confrontations with Jay Cee, her fellow young women, and physics and chemistry, is a struggle with a male domination expressed not only in social intercourse but in the potencies of language itself. The crisis, therefore, that precipitates Esther's suicide attempt is not surprisingly a literary crisis, a confrontation with the inadequacy of male writers to express a woman's inner self or to become instruments of that self-expression. Literature in and of itself is not a solution to the problem of women, for literature can also speak both male and female languages. The language of James Joyce partakes of precisely those qualities Esther associates with the masculine languages of Mr. Manzi, her father, and Jay Cee. It follows some physics of its own ("it was like a heavy wooden object falling downstairs" [131]). And it is written in barbed and horned letters reminiscent of the barbed-wire of German and the scorpions of science. Its grotesque shapes are "fantastic, untranslatable," and unsayable (131). They cannot reflect Esther's consciousness and are therefore repelled by it, "like faces in a funhouse mirror" (131). The letters force Esther into a mathematical relationship to them: she counts them. They are an "alphabet soup" that mocks nurture and denies fertility, making an "unpleasant dent" in her stomach (130). A string of one hundred letters without end, of words without pause, they provide no space for Esther "to crawl in between [the] black lines of print the way you crawl through a fence, and . . . go to sleep" (57). Esther will have to find her own literary language and form. This is precisely what Plath's novel does.

Esther's back-to-the-womb suicide attempt, characterized by her desire to be blanketed by a darkness that is her "own sweet shadow," engulfed by a "sleep" toward which she crawls in a reversal of the birth process, represents the ultimately fatal female retreat. The place of retreat is an exclusively female enclosure of which her retreats from chemistry and physics, from Jay Cee, from *Ladies' Day*, and finally and most critically from male literature, are lesser imitations. In *A Literature of Their Own*, Elaine Showalter describes a "female aesthetic" which bases itself upon "self-annihilation" rather than "self-realization": "retreat from the ego, retreat from the physical experience of women, retreat from the material world, retreat into separate rooms and separate cities. . . . The ultimate room of one's own is the grave" (297; cf. Spacks). In *The Bell Jar*, Plath explicitly rejects this aesthetic. She realizes that suicide cannot image or embody a female aesthetic, because it is, literally, a dead end. Therefore, though Esther's largely intuitive, spontaneous retreats lead to self-destruction, Plath's process of textual retreat, in the college/Jay Cee/*Ladies' Day* sequence and in the novel as a whole, represents a feminist discourse characterized not only by retreat but also by recovery. Also retreating, remembering, digressing, enveloping scene within scene, story within story, the text reopens discourse with the world from which it is at the same time in flight.

The first half of the novel records two separate narratives—the stories of Buddy Willard and of Esther's summer in New York City. These two stories do not mathematically equal one another. Rather they circle each other, each story expressed through imagistic mini-narratives embedded within the matrix created by the other similarly condensed story fragment. This relationship of stories, in which frame and focus, cause and effect—the elements of scientific formulation and equation—shift location and displace each other, inaugurates a dynamic antithesis to Esther's deathly inward spiraling. What begins as potentially deadly retreat, mirroring Esther's increasingly desperate and dangerous escapes, becomes, as it moves to the center of consciousness, a new, independent, and defiant context, no longer retreat but controlled and purposeful narrative, a story in its own right, moving outward rather than inward. There are no simple formulae in Plath's novel, no symbolic abbreviations (symbolism itself being a male form). Rather there are shapes and diagrams and cycles that breathe life into one another in a process so complex it extends out of fictional text into authorial biography.

To define this process is Plath's literary objective. Plath realizes that just as men require a thrust outward to connect their vision to the world, so women must also possess an energy capable of leading them out of the room-womb into the world. In the second half of her book, Plath describes this feminist discourse. The book opens with a powerful image of the energy that female literature must avoid. Though electricity does not immediately suggest the masculine, nonetheless it represents the male sexuality and power the female artist must replace with a potency of her own. "It was a queer, sultry summer, the summer they electrocuted the Rosenbergs," the narrative begins. "I'm stupid about executions. The idea of being electrocuted makes me sick. . . . It had nothing to do with me, but I couldn't help wondering what it would be like, being burned alive all along your nerves. . . . I thought it must be the worst thing in the world" (1). Esther's later experience with shock therapy confirms her worst suspicions about electrocution and reveals what it has to do with her:

Then something bent down and took hold of me and shook me like the end of the world. Whee-ee-ee-ee-ee, it shrilled, through an air crackling with blue light, and with each flash a great jolt drubbed me till I thought my bones would break and the sap fly out of me like a split plant. I wondered what terrible thing it was that I had done. . . . An old metal lamp surfaced in my mind. One of the few relics of my father's study. . . . One day I decided to move this lamp. . . . I closed both hands around the lamp and the fuzzy cord and gripped them tight. . . . Then something leapt out of the lamp . . . and I tried to pull my hands off, but they were stuck, and I screamed. (151–52)

In the context of international relations, electricity preserves social order by painfully punishing dissent. In the world of sexual relations, it is the powerful male charge that obliterates female consciousness (Esther falls asleep after her treatment), shrinking and fragmenting her identity (the "ee ee ee" recalls the earlier "Ee Gee"). Like barbed-wire it rapes her or splits her open like a vulnerable plant. Earlier Esther had a similar encounter with this male energy. Skiing for the first time, she experiences an orgasmic thrill. But the experience breaks her, splits her apart like the electrical shock, and anticipates her back-to-the-womb attempt. Skiing has this effect on Esther because it is directed and controlled by a male presence, both literally in the shape of Buddy, and metaphorically in the rough, "bruising snake of a rope" binding Esther to its phallic pull. Esther cannot dissociate herself from this rope; it never occurs to her to say no. The moment Esther aims down the slope (102), she gives herself to maleness: "I wanted to hone myself on [the] sun till I grew saintly and thin and essential as the blade of a knife." It is no accident that Esther falls when a man steps into her path. When maleness asserts its control over her life, when it interferes with her own internal zig-zagging rhythms (she pleads with Buddy that she can't go straight down because she does not even know how to zig-zag yet), Esther is endangered. And that danger is as much a consequence of control over her imagination as over her actions. She craves the wounding knife, imagines herself in its decidedly masculine terms (98–102).

Her realization of this danger insinuates itself into her consciousness as a decided alternative to the snakish rope, a fragile, threatened thread: "The lilt and boom threaded by me like an invisible rivulet in a desert of snow" (99). This thread is not yet strong enough to save her from the phallic rope, but it is the key. To experience the orgasmic moment on her own terms, and to survive it, Esther must discover a source of energy within herself as powerful as the phallic cords and ropes of male energy, yet of a female nature, a rivulet that brings nurture along with direction.

It is not that women are incapable of containing and embodying male energy. That, indeed, is their traditional function. No sooner has the book begun than Esther associates the electrical metaphor with Doreen: "Doreen wore these full-length nylon and lace jobs you could half see through, and dressing-gowns the colour of skin, that stuck to her by some kind of electricity. She had an interesting, slightly sweaty smell that reminded me of those scallopy leaves of sweet fern you break off and crush between your fingers for the musk of them" (5–6). Insofar as Doreen is associated with a female principle—

the scallopy leaves of sweet fern and a kind of intuitive quality that speaks straight from Esther's bones (7)—this electricity is all right; and Esther is attracted to Doreen "like a magnet" (5). But Doreen's kind of electricity is, ultimately, only an imitation of the male principle and a submission to it: her electricity leaves her painfully exposed, and it is, finally, a "marvelous, elaborate decadence" (5), giving off its scent only when the woman is crushed and broken. If nothing worse, it is static electricity and not power at all.

The female requires what Esther discovers by the end of the book: the "magical thread" that represents neither the phallus nor its erratic, spermatic electricity, but the umbilicus and the slow process of birth which it controls (cf. Coyle 173). "The deep drenched sleep," with "Doctor Nolan's face swimming" in front of her (227), quickly associates her second electric shock treatment with birth just as the earlier experience with the male chauvinist Dr. Gordon had represented a kind of death. Unlike Dr. Gordon, who confuses and mangles and veritably obliterates Esther's identity (her watch is replaced upside down, her hair pins are out of place, he greets her by repeating his earlier, sexist, identity-abbreviating comment about the WAC station, and he addresses his prognosis to Esther's mother), Dr. Nolan confirms Esther's identity and reestablishes her sense of self. She names Esther, repeating her name three times, and speaks directly to her (see Rigney's discussion of finding a name [121]). Even more important, she leads her out of the bell jar, out of the room, into the "fresh, blue-skied air" (21)—after a "brief series of five" sessions, Esther is given "town privileges" (228). And once in the world, Esther can begin to function not only as a person but as a woman (Dr. Nolan also signs her prescription for a diaphragm). The male symbols around which she had constructed a self-destructive identity suddenly lose their importance and are replaced by female symbols of freedom and control:

I took up the silver knife and cracked off the cap of my egg. Then I put down the knife and looked at it. I tried to think what I had loved knives for, but my mind slipped from the noose of the thought and swung, like a bird, in the centre of empty air. (228)

The knife had represented suicide in a double sense. Not only was it as effective a method of suicide as a noose (though both, significantly, cannot work for her), but it had represented the male image of orgasm in the skiing scene. Now it loses its importance and is replaced by the free-swinging and bird-like thread of thought. . . .

In her final pages, Plath creates a last, quintessential female image that surfaces and quickens in the dynamic process which she believes distinguishes the female aesthetic from the male. Chapter twenty begins with a long, convoluted sentence, a non sequitur to the final words of the preceding chapter. This sentence introduces a chapter replete with non-sentences, broken paragraphs and thoughts, and textual spaces, a typographical manifestation of the principles of spacing and enveloping that have characterized the novel from the beginning, as if the text itself were coming out from under the bell jar. This circling and circulating sentence gives birth to the final image of the book, "the heart of winter":

A fresh fall of snow blanketed the asylum—not a Christmas sprinkle, but a man-high January deluge, the sort that snuffs out schools and offices and churches, and leaves, for a day or more, a pure, blank sheet in place of memo pads, date books and calendars. . . .

The heart of winter. (249)

The "heart of winter" image, with its "*man*-high deluge" of obliterating snow is potentially just as dangerous as the fig tree—both for what it symbolizes about the world and for its power to assert itself as a symbol. But the heart of winter, while capable of freezing, will not itself be frozen. Able to still the world, it will not be stilled. The snow is only the heart's agent. The important figure is the heart, which represents repetition, recirculation, and remembering:

I remembered everything.

I remembered the cadavers and Doreen and the story of the fig-tree and Marco's diamond and the sailor on the Common and Doctor Gordon's wall-eyed nurse and the broken thermometers and the negro with his two kinds of beans and the twenty pounds I gained on insulin and the rock that bulged between sky and sea like a grey skull.

Maybe forgetfulness, like a kind snow, should numb and cover them.

But they were part of me. They were my landscape. (250)

The heart of winter does not obliterate the "topography" of the world that lies beneath it. Its snow blankets the pricks and stings and surfaces of this man's world, and enables them to be tolerated. But unlike the male medicine that deceives women into reproducing by annihilating their memory of pain, the heart of winter encourages birth by verifying and validating the pain, by making it an expression of meaningful consciousness. In this way it overrides the suicidal impulse, which, in its intensification of the wish to forget, becomes an acquiescence to male domination over female memory and consciousness. It replaces the desire for death, the desire to return to womb-like unconsciousness, with a desire for life, a desire to leave the womb and be born:

> There would be a black, six-foot gap hacked in the hard ground. That shadow would marry this shadow, and the peculiar, yellowish soil of our locality seal the wound in the whiteness, and yet another snowfall erase the traces of newness in Joan's grave.
>
> I took a deep breath and listened to the old brag of my heart.
>
> I am, I am, I am. (256)

The repetitive beat of her heart asserts both identity (I) and existence (am). Its triple repetition recalls Dr. Nolan's naming of Esther three times. It signals not only the fact of Esther's rebirth but the rhythm that will define it and the power that will control it. The beat or brag is not, like an electrical, spermatic charge (or even like a literal birth), a one-time expulsion of self outward. It is a continuous, repeating, loving pulsation that heals and births in the same process. And the force that supervises it is the self. Esther causes her own deep breath and listens to her own heart.

Esther's rebirth, therefore, is a self-birth. But it is also a marriage of the heart. In leaving the security of the womb, she weds herself to the world, the same world that has caused her so much pain. Picking up the car imagery that a few pages earlier signified her liberation from Buddy, Esther acknowledges that all psychological or emotional birth is rebirth, all identity a wedding of old and new. She is now "patched, retreaded and approved for the road" (257). Esther realizes that she cannot be born anew. But she can be healed. She can be born "twice" (256). The male world and its language (the world and language of cars and automotive power, for example) cannot be discarded. Indeed, they are as indispensable to female art as is male sexuality to female procreation. Plath rejects the lesbian alternative, just as she rejects the possibility of androgyny, explicitly dissociating herself from Joan and then sealing off the lesbian option in Joan's death. The topography of sexual conflict cannot be made to disappear. The sexist language exists as a part of the woman's literary and cultural heritage as surely as it forms the physical, chemical, botanical basis of the universe.

But a woman can, and must, even as she weds herself to a male world, also marry herself to her own female self. This is what Plath calls being ret(h)readed. As Dr. Nolan's touch, thread-like, draws Esther into the room, she discovers the magical thread that is both the source of her inner creativity and her link with the world. The thread moves in two directions. On the one hand, it emanates from the doctors (including the male doctors) who guide her into health and whose knowledge, experience, and language she must absorb. But it is also a thread spun out of self; it is she herself who fixes their gaze upon her and enables the thread to materialize.[4]

This thread leads out of the bell jar, out of the room of one's own, into a room that is, and perhaps will remain, largely a male space. It is a powerful thread, an umbilicus able to assimilate the male energy, to convert it within the interior space of the female into a thriving, pulsating, vibrating life, and then to bear that issue outward into the world as a unique expression of self. This is the thread of feminist discourse, which, necessarily rooting itself in the male language that has preceded it, transforms it into a feminist language and art.

## Note
4. David Holbrook cites as a "central theme" of the book "impingement . . . 'being done to'" (65–66). Here, finally, Plath is not done to, but does.

## Works Cited
Aird, Eileen. *Sylvia Plath: Her Life and Work*. New York: Harper, 1972.
Allen, May. *The Necessary Blackness: Women in Major American Fiction of the Sixties*. Urbana: U of Illinois P, 1976.
Bevilacqua, Winifred Farrant, ed. *Fiction by American Women: Recent Views*. New York: Associated Faculty, 1983.
Coyle, Susan. "Images of Madness and Retrieval: An Exploration of Metaphor in *The Bell Jar*." *Studies in Fiction* 12 (1984): 161–74.
Furman, Nelly. "The Politics of Language: Beyond the Gender Principle?" Greene and Kahn 59–79.
Gilbert, Sandra M. "What Do Feminist Critics Want: A Postcard from the Volcano." Showalter, *New Feminist* 29–45.
Greene, Gayle, and Coppelia Kahn, eds. *Making a Difference: Feminist Literary Criticism*. London: Methuen, 1985.
Heilbrun, Carolyn. *Toward a Recognition of Androgyny*. New York: Knopf, 1973.
Holbrook, David. *Sylvia Plath: Poetry and Existence*. London: Althone, 1976.
Janeway, Elizabeth. "Women's Literature." *Harvard Guide to Contemporary American Writing*. Ed. Daniel Hoffman. Cambridge: Harvard UP, 1979. 342–95.
Jones, Ann Rosalind. "Inscribing Femininity: French Theories of the Feminine." Greene and Kahn 80–112.
———. "Writing the Body: Toward an Understanding of *l'Écriture feminine*." Showalter, *New Feminist* 361–77.
Juhasz, Suzanne. *Naked and Fiery Forms: Modern American Poetry by Women*. New York: Harper, 1976.

Kroll, Judith. *Chapters in a Mythology: The Poems of Sylvia Plath*. New York: Harper, 1976.

Perloff, Marjorie. "'A Ritual for Being Born Twice': Sylvia Plath's *The Bell Jar*." Bevilacqua 101–12+.

Plath, Aurelia Schober, ed. *Sylvia Plath: Letters Home*. New York: Harper, 1975.

Plath, Sylvia. *The Bell Jar*. London: Faber, 1963.

Reardon, Joan. "*Fear of Flying*: Developing the Feminist Novel." Bevilacqua 131–43 and 157–58.

Rigney, Barbara Hill. *Madness and Sexual Politics in the Feminist Novel: Studies in Brontë, Woolf, Lessing, and Atwood*. Madison: U of Wisconsin P, 1978.

Showalter, Elaine. "Feminist Criticism in the Wilderness." Showalter, *New Feminist* 243–70.

———. *A Literature of Their Own: British Women Novelists from Brontë to Lessing*. Princeton: Princeton UP, 1972.

———. "Toward a Feminist Poetics." Showalter, *New Feminist* 125–43.

———, ed. *The New Feminist Criticism: Essays on Women, Literature, and Theory*. New York: Pantheon, 1985.

Spacks, Patricia Meyer. *The Female Imagination*. New York: Knopf, 1975.

Whittier, Gayle M. "The Divided Woman and Generic Doubleness in *The Bell Jar*." *Women's Studies* 3 (1976): 127–46.

## DIANE S. BONDS ON ESTHER'S TENTATIVE REBIRTH

Despite the ambiguities of the closing of *The Bell Jar*, critics have been surprisingly willing to accept that Esther is in some positive sense "reborn" even if her future is uncertain. In the final episode, when Esther readies herself to meet the board of doctors who will certify her release from the hospital, she behaves as if she is preparing for a bridegroom or a date; she checks her stocking seams, muttering to herself "Something old, something new. . . . But," she goes on, "I wasn't getting married. There ought, I thought, to be a ritual for being born twice—patched, retreaded, and approved for the road, I was trying to think of an appropriate one. . . ." Critics who have been willing to see a reborn Esther have generally done so without ever questioning the propriety of the reference to a "retread" job.[6] Linda Wagner, for example, ignores this passage and concentrates on subsequent paragraphs, where the image of an "open door and Esther's ability to breathe are," Wagner writes, "surely positive images."[7] Susan Coyle writes that the tire image "seems to be accurate, since the reader does not have a sense of [Esther] as a brand-new, unblemished tire but of one that has been painstakingly reworked, remade"; Coyle claims that Esther has taken steps that "however tentative, do lead her toward an authentic self that was previously impossible for her."[8] Not only do the comments of Coyle and Wagner ignore the implication of choosing the tire image in the first place; they also miss an affinity of the passage with one . . . in which Esther views wifehood in terms of service as a kitchen mat. The tire, like a kitchen mat, presents us with a utilitarian object, easily repaired or replaced, as a metaphor for a woman. It is worth observing that a patched, retreaded tire may be ready for the road, but somewhere down the highway the owner can expect a flat. Now "flatten out" is exactly what Esther suspects—or had suspected—women do in marriage. Yet it is precisely for marriage that Esther seems confusedly to be preparing herself in the final episode as she straightens her seams. It is true that she withdraws her reference to marriage, but despite her disclaimer, it seems to me, a retread job can only be a travesty of rebirth.

The metaphor of rebirth or a second birth is thus especially suspicious because of the way in which the tire image obliquely forces us to associate Esther's new lease on life with role expectations that contributed to her breakdown in the first place: the domestic servitude that Esther painfully recognizes "as a dreary and wasted life for a girl with fifteen years of straight A's." Although Esther's breakdown may have sources lying buried in the past along with her father, the novel makes it sufficiently clear that she is torn apart by the intolerable conflict between her wish to avoid domesticity, marriage and motherhood, on the one hand, and her inability to conceive of a viable future in which she avoids that fate, on the other.

Plath's inability to resolve that conflict in her own life is well known. In an essay entitled "Sylvia Plath's 'Sivvy' Poems: A Portrait of the Poet as a Daughter," Marjorie Perloff concludes:

The first shock of recognition produced by Sylvia Plath's 'independence' from her husband and her mother was the stimulus that gave rise to the *Ariel* poems. But given the 'psychic osmosis' between herself and Aurelia Plath . . . given the years of iron discipline during which Sylvia had been her mother's Sivvy, the touching assertion [in "Medusa"] that 'There is nothing between us' could only mean that now there would be nothing at all.[9]

Whatever the biographical validity of Perloff's argument, it may help us to define a pattern that has not been discerned in *The Bell Jar*. Esther's movement toward her breakdown entails a series of rejections of or separations from women who, though they may be associated with some stereotype of womanhood unacceptable to Esther, have nurtured some important aspect of her evolving identity; as I want to show, the supposed cure which she undergoes is actually a continuation of a pattern in which Esther severs relations precisely with those whose presence "in" her self has been constitutive. Such a series of rejections may dramatize a deluded notion that an autonomous and "authentic" self may be derived through purging the self of the influence of others, but there is good reason to suppose that the process actually means that little or nothing would remain to Esther, as means of modeling identity, except forms of womanhood offered to her by the very stereotypes she has sought to elude. The irony here is that in the attempt to avoid dismemberment, disfiguration or mutilation of the self, the heroine undergoes a process of self-dismemberment.

The novel provides another metaphor for the process I am describing in the repeated binge-and-purge episodes of the first portion of the novel. In chapter 2, Esther vicariously participates in Doreen's debauch with Lenny, then returns to the hotel and a bath of purification; the pattern is repeated when Doreen returns, to pass out in a pool of her own vomit. Chapter 4 presents another purgative cleansing; after gorging on caviar at a luncheon, Esther is leveled by food poisoning, an experience which makes her feel "purged and holy and ready for a new life." Shortly after this purgation, she announces: "I'm starving."

In somewhat a similar manner, I am arguing, Esther embraces relations with most of the women in the novel only to cast them off, as if they constituted a foreign presence within the purity of her own identity, some threat to her integrity. Doreen, for example, speaks to her with a voice "like a secret voice speaking straight out of [her] own bones," but after the evening in Lenny's apartment, Esther decides to have nothing to do with her. A similar pattern is repeated with every female character in the novel, including Dr. Nolan, the psychiatrist who brings about Esther's recovery, and Esther's mother.

Esther's aversion from her mother is obvious, ascending in stridency from the mild understatement, "My own mother wasn't much help" to the murderous fantasy inspired by sharing a room with her mother: one sleepless night, after staring at "the pin curls on her [mother's] head glittering like a row of little bayonets," Esther comes to feel that the only way she can escape the annoying sound of her mother's faint snore "would be to take the column of skin and sinew from which it rose and twist it to silence between [her] hands." Even though Esther at one point wishes that she had a mother like Jay Cee, the editor for whom she works at *Ladies' Day*, her ambivalence toward Jay Cee and other women who have nurtured her talents is profound—and it appears to derive, quite simply, from their supposed unattractiveness to men. Of Jay Cee, Esther says ". . . I liked her a lot. . . . [She] had brains, so her plug-ugly looks didn't seem to matter"; but sentences later, after admitting that she cannot imagine Jay Cee in bed with her husband, Esther changes her attitude abruptly: "Jay Cee wanted to teach me something, all the old ladies I ever knew wanted to teach me something, but I suddenly didn't think they had anything to teach me." A similar reflection recurs near the end of the novel in a scene where the lesbian Joan Gilling lounges on Esther's bed in the asylum and Esther's revery seems to lump the unattractive, the manless, and the woman-loving together. She remembers:

... the famous woman poet at my college [who] lived with another woman—a stumpy old Classical scholar with a cropped Dutch cut. When I told the poet that I might well get married and have a pack of children someday, she stared at me in horror. "But what about your *career*?" she had cried.

My head ached. Why did I attract these weird old women: There was the famous poet, and Philomena Guinea, and Jay Cee, and the Christian Scientist lady, and lord knows who, and they all wanted to adopt me in some way, and, for the price of their care and influence, have me resemble them.

This passage focuses our attention on the immersion of Plath/Esther in what Adrienne Rich has called the "compulsory heterosexuality," the pervasive heterosexism, of our culture.[10] It also reinforces our awareness that despite her intelligence, imagination and professional ambition, Esther's sense of identity as a woman is predicated on finding "the right man."

That Esther categorizes Jay Cee, Philomena Guinea, and the woman poet at college (who is never named)—along with the Christian Scientist lady whom she does not know—as weird old women who want to save her is a way of rejecting these women's very real contributions and potential contributions to her own evolving identity. The claim would seem to be at least partly a projection of her own desire to be saved from becoming like these women with whom she shares certain talents, capacities, and interests. I want to suggest that there may be a kind of psychic dismemberment signified by the separation of self thus from one's nurturers; denying their influence is like peeling off layers of her own self—or cutting off important members. It is especially important to notice in this regard that the point where Esther turns her back on Jay Cee coincides with the diminishment of her sense of competence, which becomes increasingly worse as the weeks pass in New York. In rejecting the "weird old women" who want to save her, she appears to become increasingly disempowered; that is, she appears to lose touch with the talents and skills that these women nurtured.

Esther's recovery involves a reinstitution of the problems that led to her breakdown. If, as I have already suggested, the reconstructed Esther is a retreaded tire doomed to go flat (and probably on the same highway that brought her to the asylum in the first place), that is partly because her cure perpetuates the disease. The recovery process of this heroine merely extends the series of separations from or rejections of others which seems to have played an important part in bringing about her breakdown.

By the closing pages of the novel, two meaningful relations with women are open to Esther, relations with her friend, Joan Gilling, and her psychiatrist, Dr. Nolan. The first of these relations is terminated decisively by the character's suicide, which renders irreversible Esther's prior rejection of that character. In the penultimate scene of the novel, Esther attends Joan's funeral, wondering, she tells us, "what I thought I was burying" and listening to the insistent "brag of [her own] heart"—"I am, I am, I am." Since Esther springs to new life as Joan is buried, it would be difficult not to conclude that Plath is putting aside, burying, some unacceptable part of her heroine: Esther has even explicitly identified Joan as "the beaming double of my old best self." Like the metaphor of a retread, however, this comment exemplifies "the uncertainty of tone" that, according to Rosellen Brown, "manages to trivialize . . . [the novel's] heavy freight of pain."[11] If the passage hints Esther's awareness that her "old best self" is peculiarly vulnerable to disintegration precisely because of the intolerable psychic conflict produced by trying to meet cultural expectations of women, it also—to the extent that it is sarcastic—distances Esther from Joan and from the painful feelings that she shares with Joan.

Until the revelation that Joan is involved in a lesbian relationship, that young woman is associated with a potential for intimacy that seems more positive than negative. Joan replaces, as Esther's neighbor, Miss Norris, with whom Esther shares an hour of "close, sisterly silence." Joan's intimacy with Dee Dee is associated with improving health (*pace* Vance Bourjaily, who writes that a "relapse" is indicated by

Joan's "lesbian involvement"[12]—the novel simply contradicts this). Esther even feels free to curl up on Joan's bed on first encountering her at one asylum, though she admits to having known Joan at college only "at a cool distance."

After discovering Joan with Dee Dee, however, Esther's treatment of Joan begins to be marked by a blatant cruelty, as when Esther tells Joan, "'I don't like you. You make me want to puke, if you want to know.'" A less explicit cruelty, implicating not merely the character Esther but the author Plath, pervades the scene where Joan seeks medical attention for Esther's hemorrhaging after Esther's encounter with Irwin. Esther/Plath clearly has one eye on humiliating Joan. Because Joan is allowed to surmise that the bleeding is some mysterious menstrual problem rather than connected to Esther's loss of virginity, she is made to look like a bumbler. She has difficulty explaining the problem clearly enough to get emergency aid, a problem which of course increases the danger to Esther, but a pun seems more important here than prompt medical assistance. When Joan asks about the man who has dropped Esther off, Esther says: "I realized that she honestly took my explanation at face value . . . and his appearance [was] a mere prick to her pleasure at my arrival." The oddity of her mentioning, in circumstances where every beat of her heart "pushed forth another gush of blood," Joan's pleasure at her arrival is matched by what looks like a kind of desperation to hide from Joan the cause of the hemorrhaging.

The peculiarities of this scene create ambiguities about Esther's motives and suggest confusion on Plath's part. Still Plath's imagery hints at a causal link between Esther's hemorrhaging and Joan's death. Often described before this episode in terms of horse imagery, Joan is here described as a "myopic owl" in an image that appears paradoxically to reveal what it intends to obscure: Joan's knowledge of the cause of Esther's suffering and the trauma of the rejection that Esther's suffering represents. Similarly, the structuring of the narrative implies a link between Joan's death and Esther's rebirth. Before she gets to the Emergency Room, Esther remembers "a worrisome course in the Victorian novel where woman after woman died, palely and nobly, in torrents of blood, after a difficult childbirth." The birth that is brought about here, however, is not that of a strong new self but of an Esther who gives in to her fear of the love and nurturance of women—exemplified by Joan's role as nurse in this scene—an Esther who buries her capacity for identification with women and accepts the very stereotypes which have been the source of her pain.

As "the only purely imagined event in the book,"[13] the inclusion of Joan's unexpected and unprepared for suicide immediately following this episode, is, as Paula Bennett has written, "necessitated not by the novel's plot, themes, or characters but by Plath's own emotional understanding of her text. Joan, the woman who loves other women and who, therefore, can pursue a career and independent life without benefit of men or marriage, must be disposed of if the demons that haunt Plath's/Esther's mind are to be exorcised as well. . . ."[14] The nature of those demons may partly be implied by the descriptions of the lesbians in the novel: not only the "stumpy" old Classical scholar, already mentioned, but the "matronly-breasted senior, homely as a grandmother and a pious Religion major, and a tall, gawky freshman with a history of being deserted at an early hour in all sorts of ingenious ways by her blind dates." Such images indicate the "weirdness," the unattractiveness, to Plath of any female behavior deviating from heterosexual, patriarchal norms: Esther says of Joan, "It was like observing a Martian, or a particularly warty toad."

It seems a kind of narrative reaction to these images that in the episode following those in which they occur, Esther has herself fitted with a diaphragm. So compelling is the logic of her desire to avoid pregnancy that we do not feel spurred to ask why she would at this point want to have anything to do with a man in the first place. But it should be noted that her encounters with men have been nearly devastating: her father deserts her by dying when she is very young; much more recently in the novel, she is knocked down in the mud, mauled, practically raped by a man who marks her face with blood; in another, a flashback to an occasion where she ends up inspecting Buddy Willard's genitals, all she can think of is "turkey neck and turkey gizzards." The man she sets out to seduce (Constantin) falls asleep unaroused by her, and the male psychiatrist to whom she turns for help practically electrocutes her. This pattern of pain and disappointment is merely confirmed by her experience with Irwin, who creates for her, in deflowering her, a possibly life-threatening medical emergency.

It is a sad irony that precisely at the point in *The Bell Jar* where the action seems to call for at least a temporary turning away from men or from seeing herself in relation to male sexuality, if only to provide for some period of reflection and healing on Esther's part, the novel turns more decisively than ever away from women and toward men. Critics have not, however, generally recognized this irony; the typical reaction has been to accept at face value that the purchase of a diaphragm is an important step in the direction of independence. While contraception surely frees Esther from fears which no women should have to suffer, my argument is that we need to question the validity of the notion of independence offered through this episode.

In killing off Joan, Plath cancels for Esther the possibility of tenderness—outside the relatively impersonal therapeutic relationship—clearly symbolized by Joan's lesbianism. That possibility is named by Dr. Nolan, the only character in the novel treated with unambiguous respect. When Esther asks this psychiatrist "What does a woman see in a woman that she can't see in a man," Dr. Nolan replies with one definitive, authoritative word: "Tenderness." Plath dramatizes both the yearning for tenderness in Esther and the way in which Esther is cut off from that yearning, but there seems to be little authorial awareness of the disjunction. The novel presents the possibility of tenderness between women in a story Esther recounts about two "suspected" lesbians at her college: "'Milly was sitting on the chair and Theodora was lying on the bed, and Milly was stroking Theodora's hair.'" An image of this sort of caress occurs at another point in the novel, significantly in connection with a male who is probably a homosexual.[15] When

Constantin, the simultaneous interpreter whom Esther fails to seduce in New York, reaches out at the end of the evening to touch her hair she feels "a little electric shock" and tells us: "Ever since I was small I loved feeling somebody comb my hair. It made me go all sleepy and peaceful." This touch is arguably the only tenderness Esther experiences in the novel, yet her response to the similar contact between Milly and Theodora is this: "I was disappointed. . . . I wondered if all women did with women was lie and hug."

In her aversion to Joan, Esther denies what the text nonetheless reveals: the possibility of a healing "tenderness" and "weirdness" that the relation of Joan and Dee Dee represents. As we have seen, this denial is authorially endorsed by Plath's invention of Joan's suicide. Suggesting that Joan represents Esther's "suicidal self" or—more exotically but no more helpfully—"the inverted Victorian side of Esther," critics with a Freudian orientation have linked Esther's recovery to a splitting off of an unacceptable portion of the self dramatized by Joan's suicide.[16] While a splitting off undoubtedly occurs, the nature of what is split off is ultimately ambiguous. Furthermore, *splitting off* appears to be a major symptom of the disorder from which Esther suffers. The novel dramatizes a tragic self-dismemberment in which the heroine, because of her very strengths and aspirations, appears to split off those components of herself that represent patriarchally-defined expectations of women, projecting these aspects of herself on her mother, her grandmother, Dodo Conway, Mrs. Willard, and the young women who are guest editors with her at *Ladies' Day*, especially Doreen and Betsy. Although she consciously rejects the influence of these others, she must still unconsciously be dominated by the patriarchal images of womanhood that she rejects; otherwise she would not need also to split off those qualities and impulses in herself that do *not* meet patriarchal expectations—all that goes counter to conventional femininity and is therefore "weird." These she projects upon Jay Cee. Philomena Guinea, the unnamed famous poet at her college, and finally Joan. Her systematic rejection of these leaves her quite possibly "with nothing" in the same sense that, as Perloff argues, Plath was left with nothing after rejecting the beliefs she inherited from her mother.

Dr. Nolan appears to play a special role in Esther's "cure," but several reservations about that role ought to be made. Combining the attributes of patriarchally-defined femininity and professional accomplishment, Dr. Nolan is set forth by some readers as an ideal role model for Esther, but the last thirty years have taught us to question this sort of image which can merely compound the oppression of women by leading them to assume expectations traditionally held of men as well as those held of women: Plath herself provides a highly visible example of the tragic consequences of uncritically embracing this model which encourages the belief that women can "have it all." Furthermore, the novel leaves ambiguous the extent of Nolan's contribution to the recovery. Although the trust she engenders in Esther undoubtedly counts for a great deal, the electroshock therapy and the psychic dismemberment involved in the process appear to get equal if not more credit for Esther's improvement. Finally, whatever the depth of Esther's indebtedness to Dr. Nolan, the relationship appears to be largely terminated by Esther's release from the hospital.

Thus, at the end of the novel, far from having moved in the direction of an "authentic self," Esther has been systematically separated from the very means by which such a self might be constituted: relationships with others. Her high heels and "red wool suit flamboyant as [her] plans" clearly signal a renewed and energized willingness to enter the sexual hunt that so dispirited her during her summer in New York. Esther's seeming preparation to reenter the hunt for "the right man" is accompanied by the strong suggestion that the right man is one with whom she may avoid emotional attachment. (Esther says gleefully, after realizing that Irwin's voice on the phone means nothing to her and that he has no way of getting in touch with her again, "I was perfectly free.") In other words, Esther's identity, the boundary of her self, has been secured by her isolation.

## Notes

6. Two treatments of the novel by critics skeptical about Esther's recovery are Bennett's chapter on the novel in *My Life a Loaded Gun* and Lynda K. Bundtzen, *Plath's Incarnations: Woman and the Creative Process* (Ann Arbor: The University of Michigan Press, 1983), pp. 109–56.

7. Linda W. Wagner, "Plath's *Bell Jar* as Female Bildungsroman," *Women's Studies*, 12 (1986), 64.

8. Susan Coyle, "Images of Madness and Retrieval: An Exploration of Metaphor in *The Bell Jar*," *Studies in American Fiction*, 12 (1984), 171.

9. Marjorie Perloff, "Sylvia Plath's 'Sivvy' Poems: A Portrait of the Poet as Daughter," in *Sylvia Plath: New Views on the Poetry*, ed. Gary Lane (Baltimore: Johns Hopkins, 1979), p. 175.

10. See Adrienne Rich, "Compulsory Heterosexuality and Lesbian Existence" in *Blood, Bread and Poetry: Selected Prose, 1979–1985* (New York: Norton, 1986), pp. 23–75.

11. Rosellen Brown, "Keeping the Self at Bay," in *Ariel Ascending: Writings About Sylvia Plath*, ed. Paul Alexander (New York: Harper, 1985), p. 122.

12. Vance Bourjaily, "Victoria Lucas and Elly Higginbottom," in *Ariel Ascending*, ed. Paul Alexander (New York: Harper, 1985), p. 138.

13. Edward Butscher, *Sylvia Plath: Method and Madness* (New York: Seabury, 1976), p. 342. Quoted by Bennett, p. 130.

14. Bennett, p. 130.

15. Bourjaily, p. 149.

16. Christopher Bollas and Murray M. Schwartz, "Absence at the Center: Sylvia Plath and Suicide," *Sylvia Plath: New Views on the Poetry*, ed. Gary Lane (Baltimore: Johns Hopkins University Press, 1979), p. 200; Gordon Lameyer, "The Double in Sylvia Plath's *The Bell Jar*," *Sylvia Plath: The Woman and the Work*, ed. Edward Butscher (New York: Dodd, 1977), p. 159.

## PAULA BENNETT ON MODELS OF WOMANHOOD

Plath's *Bell Jar* is a book about women.[11] More specifically, it is a book about growing up as a woman in a culture that is fundamentally unfair and hypocritical in its inequality. Through most of the novel, Esther, sick unto death of her good girl image but unwilling or unable to shed it, flounders in a hate-filled void: despising women because they comply

103

with a system that divides and exploits them, despising men because they claim and exercise the benefits of a superiority not truly theirs, despising herself above all for having no way out of this dilemma. Esther's quest for a woman who can show her how to resolve this conflict successfully is one of the novel's major themes. Her goal is to find a means to be both feminine and equal, that is, to be socially acceptable as a woman while still retaining her power as an autonomous individual and a potential professional. Her dilemma is resolved, however factitiously, in the final section of the novel through her contact with Dr. Nolan, the "good mother," and through her acquisition of a diaphragm, the contraceptive device that will presumably allow her to exercise her femininity without fear of accidentally falling under the domination of a man by becoming pregnant and therefore dependent, as, in effect, Plath's mother did.

Esther's problems, according to Plath, come to a head in New York City after she has won a fashion magazine contest. Under the hot klieg lights of *Ladies' Day* more than crabmeat sours. Esther discovers that the image on which she has depended for the first nineteen years of her life is a fraud. The golden girl is ash:

> I was supposed to be having the time of my life.
> I was supposed to be the envy of thousands of other college girls just like me all over America. (BJ, 2)

But the "size-seven patent leather shoes ... bought in Bloomingdale's ... with a black patent leather belt and black patent leather pocketbook to match" leave Esther numb. So do the martinis, the dance dresses, the "anonymous young men with all-American bone structures" and all the other paraphernalia designed presumably to appeal to her femininity but appealing in fact to her developing consumer lust. (Denied the power to earn, middle-class American women in this century have been encouraged to spend in prodigious quantities, usually, as here, on items designed to make them attractive to the wage-earning male.)

Esther is supposedly fulfilling the dream for which any healthy, all-American girl would be willing to sell her soul. But having sold her soul, or at any rate, her artistic ability, Plath's heroine finds that she has received a mess of potage in return.

> We had all won a fashion magazine contest, by writing essays and stories and poems and fashion blurbs, and as prizes they gave us jobs in New York for a month, expenses paid, and piles and piles of free bonuses, like ballet tickets and passes to fashion shows and hair stylings at a famous expensive salon and chances to meet successful people in the field of our desire and advice about what to do with our particular complexions. (BJ, 3)

Although Plath never specifies why Esther goes numb in New York City, the bizarre juxtaposition in this passage of the trivial and the serious is telling. In the Madison Avenue world of *Ladies Day*, everything gets reduced to the lowest common female denominator. Famous poets and great artists, a number of whom Plath met while at *Mademoiselle*, are on a par with recipes for crabmeat and avocado salad and snappy effects with mink tails. A well-made story or hat are equally rewarded. And the rewards, no matter how demeaning, are what any girl will supposedly cherish for they are the kinds of things that make girls girls. "Instead of tests or books or grades," Sandra Gilbert writes of her own experience as a guest editor at *Mademoiselle*, ". . . they gave us *clothes*. . . . Later they gave us new hairdos; makeup cases . . . sheets and bedspreads; dances on starlit rooftops; and much, much more. On those long, hot June afternoons we sat around in our pastel, air-conditioned seminar room discussing these objects and events as if they were newly discovered Platonic dialogues."[12] The best and brightest women in Plath's and Gilbert's generation, so the Madison Avenue message read, were ultimately as seducible as any street-corner bobbysoxer with a crush on a movie star and a yen for glamour. Women were all the same underneath. They wanted to be loved.

For Esther this message comes, apparently, as a devastating shock. Under the best of circumstances, she had been insecure about her femininity. She was too tall, too brainy, and generally too awkward in many of the female graces to feel completely comfortable in her all-American, college co-ed role. Now here she was in New York City with everything a true girl was supposed to want laid out before her, hers for the taking, and she is miserable, not elated. More than that, having sacrificed a good part of her integrity for this success, she feels dirty and polluted. She no longer knows who she is. Confronted by her boss, Jay Cee, on her plans for the future, this girl who spent "nineteen years . . . running after good marks and prizes and grants" (BJ, 31) answers only "'I don't really know'" (BJ, 35). What kind of career can possibly be meaningful to a woman if women are what *Ladies Day* perceives and encourages them to be? Yet if Esther rejects the *Ladies Day* version of womanhood, supported as that version is by her mother, her college friends, the boys she dates, the experts she consults, the books she reads, the movies she sees, and the songs she hears, then who or what is she anyway?

It is this conundrum that causes Esther to grind to a halt in *The Bell Jar*. Confronted by the gulf between her gender or being and her aspirations, she is left feeling numb, stuck, as she says over and over again, in a dark, airless sack like an aborted fetus under its glass bell. Looking at the choices made by the women she knows, she can find no acceptable alternative for herself. Women either embrace the role society designates and betray themselves in the process (her mother, Mrs. Willard, Dodo, Betsy, Doreen, and the nameless girls in the college dormitory who shun Esther when she has no steady date or acts too much like a grind) or they pursue their careers, their independent lives, at the expense of their womanhood (Jay Cee with her "plug-ugly looks," the lesbian poet at Esther's college, and Joan with her horsey smell). Neither kind of woman presents Esther with a model for herself or an example she wishes to follow. At best she merely oscillates between them, listening to the advice they give but unable to follow the paths they take.

When I had told the poet [the "famous woman poet" at Esther's college who is one of her principal mentors] I might well get married and have a pack of children someday, she stared at me in horror. "But what about your *career*?" she had cried.

My head ached. Why did I attract these weird old women? There was the famous poet, and Philomena Guinea, and Jay Cee, and the Christian Scientist lady and lord knows who, and they all wanted to adopt me in some way, and for the price of their care and influence, have me resemble them. (BJ, 247–48)

Like the prototypical neurotic whom her fiancée, Buddy Willard, describes to her, the man who cannot decide whether he wants to live in the city or the country (BJ, 103–4), Esther wants two mutually exclusive things at once: marriage and a career, "a pack of children" and poetry. In her fantasies she flies back and forth between these alternatives, unable to pick one because she cannot bring herself to give up the other.

I tried to imagine what it would be like if Constantin were my husband.

It would mean getting up at seven and cooking him eggs and bacon and toast and coffee and dawdling about in my nightgown and curlers after he'd left for work to wash up the dirty plates and make the bed. . . . and I'd spend the evening washing up even more dirty places till I fell into bed, utterly exhausted.

This seemed a dreary and wasted life for a girl with fifteen years of straight A's. (BJ, 93)

In the last sentence Esther slams up against the truth that stops her every time she tries to take one of her own domestic fantasies seriously. With probably the same ingenuous spirit in which Adlai Stevenson exhorted Plath's graduating class at Smith to go out and use their education to become better wives and mothers ("We loved it," Nancy Hunter Steiner recalls),[13] Buddy Willard had told Esther that "after [she] had a child

. . . [she] wouldn't want to write poems any more." Both men were handing down the wisdom of the day, truths Esther saw moreover lived out in the daily lives of the married women around her.

> I knew that's what marriage was like, because cook and clean and wash was just what Buddy Willard's mother did from morning till night, and she was the wife of a university professor and had been a private school teacher herself. (BJ, 93)

No matter how many A's she got or how enlightened the man that she married was, if she wished to get married and have children, this would be her fate as well. Yet if she did not marry, what kind of empty, unpleasant, "plug-ugly" existence did she have to look forward to?

After her return from New York City, Esther's growing recognition of the mutual exclusivity of her goals drives her into a deeper and deeper depression. Paralleling Plath's own experience at *Mademoiselle*, the guest editorship at *Ladies Day* was supposed to have been the high point in Esther's budding career, but what it revealed to her was the hollowness of her efforts, the fact that given the society in which she lived, her aspirations were ash. After Esther comes home from New York, she can neither care for her looks, her femininity, nor pursue her studies, that is, continue to ready herself for a career. Debarred from summer school, her one tenuous hope for a meaningful summer, she lets her hair and clothing go. She stops reading. She can't write. She wonders if she is competent even to wait on tables or to type.

Esther sees herself sitting in the crotch of a fig tree, "starving to death, just because [she] couldn't make up [her] mind" which fig to choose (BJ, 85). Esther is indeed starving. Surrounded by women at school, at the women's hotel in New York, at *Ladies Day*, and in her own home, where she breathes in "the motherly breath of the suburbs" (BJ, 126) and shares a room with her mother, there is not one woman, until Dr. Nolan successfully makes contact with her, who can feed or nurture

Esther or to whom she can successfully relate. It is not simply Esther's mother who fails her, but womanhood itself.

And inevitably, therefore, Esther's anger and disillusionment with womanhood turns against herself in the ultimate act of self-destruction. If she cannot take shorthand or write novels, go on dates or read James Joyce—all activities she attempts after her return from *Ladies Day*—without debilitating internal conflict, then there is, in effect, nothing she can do. As a woman she has no clear purpose in living.

> I could see day after day after day glaring ahead of me like a white, broad, infinitely desolate avenue.
>
> It seemed silly to wash one day when I would only have to wash again the next.
>
> It made me tired just to think of it.
>
> I wanted to do everything once and for all and be through with it. (BJ, 143)

She might as well be dead.

In the final section of the novel, Plath has Dr. Nolan, the good mother, show Esther the way out of this dilemma by providing her with the long-sought model to follow. Dr. Nolan is perfectly suited to her role as surrogate parent. Unlike Esther's first psychiatrist, Dr. Gordon, the bad father, who keeps a picture of his happy family plus dog on his desk and mishandles Esther's shock treatments, Dr. Nolan is the essence of straightforward professional concern. Yet her professionalism is softened by nurturing warmth: She provides "milk" along with shock therapy. To Esther she is the one woman able to fuse femininity with intellect, an attractive appearance and manner with successful dedication to a career. The picture Esther draws of her has an almost movie star ring. Dr. Nolan steps out of a film from the late forties, fancy spectacles and all.

> I was surprised to have a woman. I didn't think they had woman psychiatrists. This woman was a cross between Myrna Loy and my mother. She wore a white blouse and

a full skirt gathered at the waist by a wide leather belt, and stylish, crescent-shaped spectacles. (BJ, 210)

Like the fairy godmother of the childhood fantasies that Plath adored (J, 20–21), Dr. Nolan is able to free the princess from the spell that holds her bound, immobilized, in place. But the sad fact is that the wand she uses is a diaphragm. Into Esther's otherwise unchanged hands, she places the instrument meant to secure Esther's sexuality while releasing her from the paralyzing fear of its consequences. Without a baby "hanging over [her] head like a big stick, to keep [her] in line," Esther believes she no longer has to fear coming "under a man's thumb" (BJ, 249). She can pursue her all-American, good girl image and her career simultaneously, confident that having one will not necessarily jeopardize the other.

To Esther the diaphragm means freedom, "freedom from fear, freedom from marrying the wrong person, like Buddy Willard, just because of sex, freedom from the Florence Crittenden Homes [for unwed mothers]" (BJ, 251). But as Lynda Bundtzen has recently noted, nowhere in the text does Plath suggest that Esther's deeper problems have been solved by the acquisition of this device or by the various forms of therapy she received along with it.[14] On the contrary, to judge by the Irwin episode, Esther's attitude toward men is, if anything, even more rigid and vindictive after her suicide attempt than it was before. Nor, as far as one can tell, has her concept of marriage or her definition of womanhood been substantially altered. Although Plath saw many of the problems connected with her view of marriage and womanhood clearly when she wrote *The Bell Jar* in 1961, she was still not prepared to deal with these issues completely then—no more than she had been able to in 1954.

At the conclusion of *The Bell Jar*, Joan, the overt lesbian and Esther's "wry, black image" (BJ, 246), hangs herself. Since Joan, who was a patient at the same hospital as Esther, was also presumably making progress, the suicide is unexpected and Plath offers no explanation for it. The inclusion of this event appears, consequently, to be a cathartic act on Plath's part, necessitated not by the novel's plot, themes, or characters but by Plath's own emotional understanding of her text. Joan, the woman who loves other women and who, therefore, can pursue a career and an independent life without benefit of men or marriage, must be disposed of if the demons that haunt Plath's/Esther's mind are to be exorcised as well. While it might seem that Joan—horsey, awkward, overly intellectual, and thoroughly unfeminine—is well got rid of by an author/protagonist about to embark upon a new, integrated life, it is a sad note of historical irony that the woman upon whom Joan Gilling is loosely based actually, according to Butscher, "went on to become a highly respected psychologist." Her suicide, he writes, is "the only purely imagined event in the book."[15]

Plath ends *The Bell Jar* with Esther exiting triumphantly stage left, bearing her diaphragm aloft while Joan, the defeated, is laid to rest beneath the pearly snow. Particularly in light of later events, this conclusion is unbearably factitious. Yet given Esther's/Plath's determination after her first breakdown to reconcile the irreconcilable—to maintain her image while still pursuing her career—it was perhaps the only option available to the author. Certainly the diaphragm brought one aspect of Esther's second-class status into line, namely the double standard. And given the society in which Esther (and Plath) lived, for the author this may well have seemed victory enough.

But beyond sexual freedom, which, according to Butscher, Plath exploited to the hilt after her return to Smith, and which, according to her *Journals*, she continued to exploit until her marriage to Hughes, Plath herself seems to have gained little from her experience at the psychiatric hospital. She returned to Smith, Butscher writes, "as disoriented as ever, still committed to disguise as a fundamental mode of behavior and composition,"[16] still, I would add, hollow and unintegrated at her core.

### Notes

11. In *Plath's Incarnations*, Lynda Bundtzen treats the novel from somewhat the same perspective but gives most of her emphasis to a Freudian interpretation. See pp. 109–56.

12. Sandra Gilbert, "A Fine, White Flying Myth: The Life/Work of Sylvia Plath," in Gilbert and Gubar, *Shakespeare's Sisters*, p. 246.

13. Steiner, *A Closer Look*, p. 109.

14. Bundtzen, *Incarnations*, pp. 114–15. As Bundtzen observes, "the real sources for [Esther's] feelings of inadequacy remain submerged and inaccessible to (her) conscious mind." By the same token, I believe they were also still largely submerged and inaccessible to Plath when she wrote *The Bell Jar*, which makes a psychoanalytic reading of the novel treacherous at best.

15. Butscher, *Method and Madness*, p. 342.

16. Butscher, *Method and Madness*, p. 136.

## PAT MACPHERSON ON THE PORTRAYAL OF SOCIAL AND GENDER CONVENTIONS

After Esther scatters her *Mlle* career-girl wardrobe over Manhattan from the roof of the Amazon hotel—perhaps her most articulate commentary on her guest-editorship—she goes home to see the other life on offer to her: suburban wife-and-mother. In no time at all she has explored the four corners of that box: the social organization of the suburb, the power relations of marriage, the medicalization of childbirth, and when all else fails, the final solution of psychiatry, defining and enforcing norms for women in relation to family. Her experience of anomie, thoroughly explained by her recognition of the oppressively reinforcing interconnections among these four social institutions, is none the less diagnosed as her own problem by Dr Gordon the psychiatrist, and treated first with pills and then with shock treatment. Her suicide attempt can be read as her critique, as a refusal, as Dr Gordon's failure to adjust her.

Esther's life at Home with Mother is the stage-set for her breakdown. While withholding all direct analysis of cause, the narrative implicitly connects Esther's constricting vision with the claustrophobia-inducing concentric circles of containment oriented, security-minded suburban regional planning. Lewis Mumford (quoted by Ada Louise Huxtable in the *New York Times Book Review*, 26 November 1989, p. 25) called the suburbs 'an asylum for the preservation of illusion', and in the

1950s, Mom stood at the centre of the illusion of security—and its breakdown.

Zipping from New York to suburban train station, the commuter is driven home in the station-wagon, the wife-and-mother having democratically replaced all domestic staff with her own All-Round personality. Esther's movement is that of the college-educated woman upon marriage.

> I stepped from the air-conditioned compartment onto the station platform, and the motherly breath of the suburbs enfolded me. It smelt of lawn sprinklers and station wagons and tennis rackets and dogs and babies.
> A summer calm laid its soothing hand over everything, like death. (126–7)

Her mother at the wheel, driving her homeward into the heart of suburban domesticity, seems to be locking the doors and throwing away the key when she announces that Esther has not won her way into a writing seminar in Boston for the summer.

> All through June the writing course had stretched before me like a bright, safe bridge over the dull gulf of the summer. Now I saw it totter and dissolve, and a body in a white blouse and green skirt plummet into the gap. (127)

The structure of school and the fuel of winning her way is the structure and fuel of Esther's psyche itself. In the suburbs this structure disappears, leaving 'large unfenced acres of time' (Plath 1983: 51) devoted solely to domestic maintenance and child-raising, with not one of the familiar supports of 'achievement' possible. Esther's feeling the suburban summer world as a gulf and gap points to its threat to her psychic as much as social identity.

Plath's journal in 1952 uses the bell jar to describe the elaborately structured, rewarded and time-managed atmosphere of her schooling, internalized as her psychic structure itself, which is then threatened with disaster when all external structure is removed:

The responsibility, the awful responsibility of managing (profitably) 12 hours a day for 10 weeks, is rather overwhelming when there is nothing, no one, to insert an exact routine into the large unfenced acres of time.... It is like lifting a bell jar off a securely clockworklike functioning community, and seeing all the little busy people stop, gasp, blow up and float in the inrush (or rather outrush) of the rarefied scheduled atmosphere. (Plath 1983: 50–1)

The bell jar here is the 'superficial and artificial' pressure to achieve in the competitive enterprise systems of school, magazine and literary world. Lift that motivational support, drive educated women into the 'dead summer world' of suburban child-rearing, and not just poor old Esther but 'all the little busy people stop, gasp, blow up . . .'

The thought of spending two weeks with two children in a close dark hole was too horrible to think of and we knew we had to do something. Now that we women have started we will no longer be content to be dull uninformed housewives. (May 1988: 208)

Nuclear war threatened a potentially explosive excess of togetherness in the family bomb shelter and rationalized the formation of the Women's Strike for Peace in 1963, as these words testify. But they also testify to the pressures women felt within the nuclear family in the suburbs, where they were in charge of security and civil defence through sound citizen-building. Dr Spock in 1945 explained this cold war maternalism: 'Useful, well-adjusted citizens are the most valuable possession a country has, and good mother care during early childhood is the surest way to produce them. It doesn't make sense to let mothers go to work' (Spock 1945: 460). Such responsibility for making the family work in the 'close dark hole' of the 'togetherness' norm is enough to induce claustrophobia—of which mothers themselves became the causes in the therapeutic and popular culture stereotypes of the smothering mother.

By assigning herself the blame for failing as a student, Esther can assign herself the appropriate punishment: a summer stuck in the suburbs, her days spent unable to read or write, her nightly entertainment a sleepless watch over her Medusa-mother's pincurls, 'glittering like a row of little bayonets' (137) in the other twin bed next to her.

Esther feels shame at having failed her college achievement test, and suggests that the suburbs are the prison to which women are sentenced—or sentence themselves:

> I felt it was very important not to be recognized.
> The gray, padded car roof closed over my head like the roof of a prison van, and the white, shining, identical clapboard houses with their interstices of well-groomed green proceeded past, one bar after another in a large but escape-proof cage.
> I had never spent a summer in the suburbs before. (127–8)

The horror at the heart of this darkness can be read in two ways at once: as Esther's self-punishing withdrawal from the social world due to the breakdown of her capacity for making meaning in her life, and as American society's punishing relegation of middle-class women to the domestic sphere, breaking down their capacities to make meaning from their education in relation to the larger social world—destroying the 'bright, safe bridge' of some career dream built to transport one's self from college to housewife. This is the reason 'why America produced the most vigorous feminist movement in the world', Barbara Ehrenreich points out: 'We were one of the only countries in which the middle class (which is wealthy by world standards) customarily employed its own women as domestic servants (Ehrenreich 1989: 40). . . .

Buddy Willard has the thankless role in *The Bell Jar* of articulating the ramifications of Esther's shrinkage from girlfriend to wife. He does this with a completely unselfconscious conviction of male superiority, necessarily accompanied by an equally complete lack of interest in and understanding of women, including Esther. His marriage offer—'How would you like to be Mrs Buddy Willard?'—tidily frames his expectations into her prospects. 'I also remembered Buddy Willard saying in a sinister, knowing way that after I had children I would feel differently, I wouldn't want to write poems any more' (94). Buddy's smug knowingness makes her wife-and-motherhood seem like a *fait accompli*. Her imagination completes the story as a sci-fi horror film: 'So I began to think maybe it was true that when you were married and had children it was like being brainwashed, and afterward you went about numb as a slave in some private, totalitarian state' (94). As for marital sex, for a sneak preview, Buddy drops his fishnet underpants, explaining, 'They're cool, and my mother says they wash easily' (75).

> Then he just stood there in front of me and I kept on staring at him. The only thing I could think of was turkey neck and turkey gizzards and I felt very depressed. (75)

What's wrong with Mr Right?

> I didn't know what to say. My mother and my grandmother had started hinting around to me a lot lately about what a fine, clean boy Buddy Willard was, coming from such a fine, clean family, and how everybody at church thought he was a model person, so kind to his parents and to older people, as well as so athletic and so handsome and so intelligent. (75)

Buddy is the all-American ideal, a 'big, broad-shouldered bonehead' type like the football hero of the movie Esther saw in New York that put her 'in terrible danger of puking' (46). You've seen the movie, now live the life. She sees the scriptedness of Buddy's lines, her mother's and grandmother's rapt approval of Buddy's good-guy image, and the inevitability of the plot line from 'roses and kisses and restaurant dinners' to the domestic 'flatten[ing] out underneath his feet like Mrs Willard's kitchen mat' (93–4). Half her objections are to her own apparently irrevocable reduction into domestic drudge—'a dreary and wasted life for a girl with fifteen years of straight A's' (93)—and half are to other women's apparent willingness to undergo this metamorphosis called marriage—'cook and clean and wash was just what Buddy Willard's mother did from morning till night, and she was the wife of a university professor and had been a private school teacher herself' (93). At the movie with her fellow guest editors, she sees romance glowing on their faces while the shadow of slavery to the totalitarian state lurks like the real moral of the story for 'stupid moonbrains' (46):

> At about this point I began to feel peculiar. I looked round me at all the rows of rapt little heads with the same silver glow on them at the front and the same black shadow on them at the back, and they looked like nothing more or less than a lot of stupid moonbrains. (46)

The Happy Ending was promised but left undocumented by this Big Screen romance. Esther has the question posed by all female adolescents: If 'a happy marriage was the happiest condition', as Elizabeth Barrett Browning said she 'vaguely believed', '—*where were the happy marriages?*' (Browning 1978: 6). The Willards are the intact family in *The Bell Jar*, Mr Willard playing 'the arrow into the future' and Mrs Willard 'the place the arrow shoots off from' (79), if Mrs Willard's model of marriage can be taken as the achieved reality of their relationship. The only thing missing is a daughter, and Mr Willard graciously offers the part of daughter-in-law to Esther. Again the Big Question reads more like a final door-slamming answer in Esther's book. Her hysterical inability to speak brings tears at the father's suggestion, and 'the awful impulse to laugh' at the son's marriage proposal (97, 102). . . .

Marriage and motherhood loom as the monstrous maternal maw, threatening to swallow up her unmaternal self, desire to express herself, and sexual desires. This totalitarian state of kitchen-mat-wifehood is the fate of Mrs Willard in *The Bell Jar*. Such an alarming possibility is mentioned as a probability by Plath's boyfriend Dick Norton, the prototype for Buddy Willard in *The Bell Jar*. Plath quotes Norton as telling her: 'I am afraid the demands of wifehood and motherhood would preoccupy you too much to allow you to do the painting and writing you want' (Plath 1983: 44). There is a crazy-making aspect to negotiating these marital expectations, which include her own ambivalences, as well as Dick Norton's idea of a doctor's wife, and both mothers' enthusiasm about the couple, which seems to support *his* version of wifehood. 'He alternately denies and accepts me, as I silently do him' (Plath 1983: 44–5), Plath writes, making clear how powerful the Other is in confirming or negating our own sense of ourselves—all within a social structure where identity comes primarily through job. The eligible woman is recognized by her education, accepted as a professional for the equal-partners companionate marriage. Then her professional identity is denied in the domestic sphere. Her sexual equality is denied before marriage, accepted after. Now you see her, now you don't. On her part, such acceptance and denial of him is done 'silently', totally subverting all her potential power to shape *his* identity-through-relationship. They're not arguing, after all, about what a man is or does or wants or needs or gets in marriage. The burden is all on her to resist, redefine and convince—without, of course, being 'strong and assertive'. 'So [Dick] accuses me of "struggling for dominance"? Sorry, wrong number. . . . It is only *balance* that I ask for. Not the *continual* subordination of one person's desires and interests to the continual advancement of another's! That would be too grossly unfair' (Plath 1983: 43). This grossly unfair continual subordination of the wife-and-mother to Family was defined as femininity itself in the 1950s. . . .

Having rejected Buddy Willard's invitation to the Happy Family, Esther finds him waiting for her in the hospitals to which she is sent. There he bears on his broad shoulders the burden of all paternalism controlling the professions, especially science and medicine, as they justify conventionality using large doses of clinical rationality. After Esther's anomie, such certitude has its attractions.

[His] mind, she was certain, would be flat and level, laid out with measured instruments in the broad, even sunlight. There would be geometric concrete walls and square, substantial buildings with clocks on them, everywhere perfectly in time, perfectly synchronized. The air would be thick with their accurate ticking. (Plath 1980: 301)

Plath's bell jar image from her journal haunts this passage from 'Sunday Morning at the Mintons'. Plath's story, published in *Mlle* in 1952, celebrates the triumphant flight of female imagination over such male flat-footed certitude. But ten years later in *The Bell Jar*, by setting such men as Buddy Willard in their institutional contexts of hospital and happy family, Plath shows the social power that makes his cartoonish balloon-speeches into the punishing particulars of female patienthood, whether obstetrical or psychiatric. 'It is so', proclaims the silver hair in its boyish crewcut, the clear blue eyes, the pink cheeks (97). 'If you think so', rebelliously thinks the dutiful daughter. 'I think we understand each other' (97) he finishes, turning misrecognition into male knowledge with a satisfied sigh.

The photo of the wife-and-kids on the psychiatrist's desk does all the talking for Doctor Gordon during Esther's sessions with him. When that fails to enable Esther to snap out of it, he applies 'his private shock machine. Once I was locked up they could use that on me all the time' (179) she accurately predicts—and furiously undertakes yet another frustrated suicide attempt, in classic female fashion. Electroshock treatments, like delivery-room anaesthetics, like tranquilizers, were popularized in the 1950s with largely the same rationale for largely the same clientele. Buddy assures Esther that the woman giving birth

really didn't know what she was doing because she was in a kind of twilight sleep . . . on a drug that would make her forget she'd had any pain.

I thought it sounded just like the sort of drug a man would invent. Here was a woman in terrible pain,

119

obviously feeling every bit of it or she wouldn't groan like that, and she would go straight home and start another baby, because the drug would make her forget how bad the pain had been, when all the time, in some secret part of her, that long, blind, doorless and windowless corridor of pain was waiting to open up and shut her in again. (72)

'That's what I heard—that's what everybody tells you—that it's to make you forget' (Warren 1987: 133) explained 'Rita', a woman given shock treatments. Carol Warren's study *Madwives* (1987) re-examines the medical records and interviews of a group of women in a California hospital in the 1950s, and draws firm connections between the isolation of suburban housewives and depression, and between husbands and hospitals and technology coordinating an oppressive social control of women. Another woman explained the desired result: after shock treatments 'I wasn't depressed or despondent. . . . Now, I don't feel anything' (Warren 1987:135). 'Rita' said her shock treatments 'made me forget some things, but not enough. I haven't had enough, I guess' (Warren 1987:133). Medical technology refined the behavioural control of women patients under the principle of adjustment toward normalcy. More than one woman interpreted her treatment and even her depression as her punishment for deviancy, for failure to fulfil her role—or, even more shameful, for failing to *want* to fulfil her role. Taking the blame for breakdown is halfway back to normalcy, accepting one's responsibility to adjust oneself. . . .

Esther's gruesome tour of the hospital with Buddy the medical student, her poorly played imitation of a volunteer nurse on the maternity ward at the local hospital, and her painfully mishandled shock treatments at Doctor Gordon's suburban clinic for depressed housewives, gradually move Esther toward the experience of involuntary institutionalization, the ultimate female subjection to male control of knowledge and technology. Plath remembered the film *The Snake Pit*, and feared the tunnels under the hospital, through which the patients get wheeled to that intimate mating of their nerves with Dr Frankenstein's lightning machine, the marriage of their accumulated pain with all the wisdom of male science.

## TIM KENDALL ON ESTHER'S SEARCH FOR IDENTITY

Plath's inability to fit any of the acceptable roles defined by her social and educational background seems to have been a major cause of her first breakdown in 1953. Esther, in *The Bell Jar*, faces a similar dilemma, as the novel very soon makes clear:

> I was supposed to be having the time of my life.
>
> I was supposed to be the envy of thousands of other college girls just like me all over America who wanted nothing more than to be tripping about in those same size seven patent leather shoes I'd bought in Bloomingdale's one lunch hour with a black patent leather belt and black patent leather pocket-book to match. And when my picture came out in the magazine the twelve of us were working on—drinking martinis in a skimpy, imitation silver-lamé bodice stuck on to a big fat cloud of white tulle, on some Starlight Roof, in the company of several anonymous young men with all-American bone structures hired or loaned for the occasion—everybody would think I must be having a real whirl.
>
> Look what can happen in this country, they'd say. A girl lives in some out-of-the-way town for nineteen years, so poor she can't afford a magazine, and then she gets a scholarship to college and wins a prize here and a prize there and ends up steering New York like her own private car.
>
> Only I wasn't steering anything, not even myself. (BJ, 2/2)

Esther's competitive nature and her will to succeed become frustrated, not satisfied, by her conspicuous achievements. The goal she aims for, once attained, seems tawdry and artificial, her life a charade: even the dress is 'imitation silver-lamé'.

121

Later Esther sits through a technicolor romance starring a 'nice blonde girl who looked like June Allyson but was really somebody else, and a sexy black-haired girl who looked like Elizabeth Taylor but was also somebody else, and two big, broad-shouldered bone-heads with names like Rick and Gil' (BJ, 43/42–43). In this world where everyone strives to be 'somebody else', and where morality and identity go no deeper than the superficialities of Hollywood, Esther has no trouble foreseeing the denouement: the nice girl will end up with the nice football hero and the sexy girl will end up with nobody, 'because the man named Gil had only wanted a mistress and not a wife all along and was now packing off to Europe on a single ticket'. Appropriately, Esther is taken ill before the end of the film, having fallen victim to the hospitality of her magazine's 'Food Testing Kitchens'. The food which had looked good enough to photograph for the housewives of America is not good enough to eat. Esther discovers that the spotless hygiene of 1950s technicolor America is a façade which may conceal an unhealthy reality—it may even make you sick.

*The Bell Jar* is a novel about the searching for and shedding of identity, just as Esther sheds the contents of her wardrobe from her hotel roof. She calls herself Elly Higginbottom, and invents a history for herself as an orphan from Chicago. She has never been there, but she fantasises that 'In Chicago, people would take me for what I was' (BJ, 140/132). Shorn of parents, name and roots, Esther can be her real self, even if this real self is a complete fiction. Esther imagines a world where she can fail without reproach, where nobody knows she has thrown away her education and her opportunity to marry 'a perfectly solid medical student' who will one day earn 'pots of money'. Hers is an opting out of the expectations of teachers and family. Yet her escape merely traps her in another gender stereotype: 'And one day I might just marry a virile, but tender, garage mechanic and have a big cowy family'. Appalled by the role-playing which ensures her success, and unable to find a satisfactory alternative, Esther gradually narrows down her options to just one: suicide.

Analysing a passage from the journals, Jacqueline Rose raises a question which seems just as pertinent to *The Bell Jar*: 'Plath is articulating here a problem which we can now see as fundamental for feminism. How can women assert themselves against social oppression [. . .] without propelling themselves beyond the bounds of identity, without abolishing identity itself?'[7] This is an important concern, which immediately feeds into ongoing debates about the relevance (or otherwise) of Plath's life and work for feminism. Feminist readings of *The Bell Jar* tend to side with Esther against her society, although they rarely acknowledge the difficulty of their allegiance. Accepting Esther's vision of society too credulously entails sharing her distaste at the successful, strong, professional women around her, and sharing, too, her attitudes towards heterosexual and lesbian relationships. Esther may be a misfit, but she has no sympathy for other misfits. Despite the arguments of Rose, Van Dyne and others, her crisis of identity need not (and does not) relate purely to feminism. She remains preternaturally conscious of the fact that identity, be it male or female, is for her a limiting construct, as artificial as the movies.

This awareness ensures that Esther will be unable to find, in the female characters she meets, an attractive role model. Each possibility, seemingly dangled before her like figs on a fig tree, constitutes merely another form of entrapment. Plath herself, in a journal entry from December 1958, acknowledges a 'Fear of making early choices which close off alternatives' (J, 445). For Esther, the available identities are mutually exclusive. She cannot become an innocent June Allyson clone or a vampish Elizabeth Taylor clone, in the effortless manner of Betsy and Doreen. Despite her brief thought of a big cowy family, she finds herself unable to dream of 'baby after fat puling baby like Dodo Conway'. Jay Cee and Philomena Guinea represent, in their different, repulsive ways, the woman of letters, prompting Esther to wonder why she attracts 'weird old women' who try to adopt her and make her resemble them (BJ, 232/220). Even Doctor Nolan is viewed suspiciously, as a possible betrayer; although well-intentioned, she encourages Esther on a path of sexual freedom which immediately comes close to killing her. Almost without exception, the women disgust Esther, and not only when they are conforming to male constructions of femininity: Joan's sexual advances, and her being caught in flagrante with Dee Dee, make Esther 'puke', as she carefully reiterates (BJ, 231-2/219-20).

*The Bell Jar* might even be described as a misogynistic text, were it not that the male characters are no more attractive, and no less grotesque. They range from Marco the woman-hater to bland and hypocritical Buddy Willard, the sight of whose genitalia reminds Esther of 'turkey neck and turkey gizzards' and makes her feel 'very depressed' (BJ, 71/69). The most acceptable man is Constantin, a UN interpreter, but marrying even him is a prospect almost too horrible for Esther to contemplate:

> It would mean getting up at seven and cooking him eggs and bacon and toast and coffee and dawdling about in my night-gown and curlers after he'd left for work to wash up the dirty plates and make the bed, and then when he came home after a lively, fascinating day he'd expect a big dinner, and I'd spend the evening washing up even more dirty plates till I fell into bed, utterly exhausted. (BJ, 88/84)

The rhythms of the passage mimic the rhythms of the subject: both end in breathless exhaustion. What men want from marriage, Esther maintains with characteristic overstatement, is for their wife to 'flatten out' under their feet 'like Mrs Willard's kitchen mat' (BJ, 89/85). Women are brainwashed slaves in a 'private, totalitarian state'. Even memory of the pain of childbirth, to which Plath looked forward in her letter to Richard Sassoon, is denied them by a drug invented by men (BJ, 68). Worst of all, women connive in this system. Buddy Willard constantly repeats his mother's gnomic wisdom: '"What a man is is an arrow into the future and what a woman is is the place the arrow shoots off from"' (BJ, 74/72). Plath herself, in a journal entry of late 1958, considers that '[Dick Norton's] mother was not so wrong about a man supplying direction and a woman the warm emotional power of faith and love' (J, 454)—a sentiment which might have come straight out of *Letters Home*. But Esther refuses to accept an orthodox role. She wants to 'shoot off in all directions myself, like the colored arrows from a Fourth of July rocket' (BJ, 87/83), a desire prefiguring the heat and acceleration of 'Ariel'.[8] From the novel's opening lines, it is evident that the sickness is located not just in Esther but in her society. Misanthropy becomes a form of resistance. Esther portrays herself as a victim of state control like the Rosenbergs: ECT is designed to make her conform to the same social structures which are responsible for her breakdown.

The novel's repeated references to the promise of rebirth seem to be finally realised when Esther survives and is apparently healed by her therapy; the suicide of her double, Joan Gilling, is an integral part of this symbolic pattern, allowing Esther to move on, 'patched, retreaded and approved for the road' (BJ, 257/244). But this metaphor of Esther patched like an old tyre suggests the need to continue with the battered old self rather than acceding to a glorious new one. Even such limited optimism remains precarious: 'How did I know', Esther asks, 'that someday—at college, in Europe, somewhere, anywhere—the bell jar, with its stifling distortions, wouldn't descend again?' (BJ, 254/241). She has reason to feel concerned, because the novel offers her no form of reconciliation with society. Her regular references to 'what I really am' (BJ, 77/74) are soon undercut. Within a few lines she can shift from identification with the good and conformist Betsy—'It was Betsy I resembled at heart'—to an imaginative alliance with wicked non-conformist Doreen: 'I think I still expected to see Doreen's body lying there in the pool of vomit like an ugly, concrete testimony to my own dirty nature' (BJ, 24/23). Esther contains all and none of the multitudes presented to her, and in terms of discovering an underlying stable identity, remains as faceless at the end of the novel as at the beginning.

*The Bell Jar* does allow at least the possibility that Esther will, eventually, discover a role which satisfies her. Early on, she remembers the free gifts she received during her time at the magazine: 'For a long time afterwards I hid them away, but later, when I was all right again, I brought them out, and I still have them around the house. I use the lipsticks now and then, and last week I cut the plastic starfish off the sunglasses case for the baby to play with' (BJ, 3–4/3). Later, in a reference to pregnancy which is both coy and gratuitous, Esther declares that 'With one exception I've been the same weight for ten years' (BJ, 25/24). The motivation for these narrative devices is primarily reassurance: however terrible the breakdown which the reader is about to witness, they guarantee a safe conclusion. Barring the unlikely possibility of posthumous narration (a possibility which Plath does exploit in 'The Rabbit Catcher'), the first-person voice makes it immediately obvious that Esther has lived to tell her tale. The emphasis on fertility as the barometer of Esther's mental health also indicates the distance she has travelled since the trauma of watching Mrs Tomolillo's labour and episiotomy, and since declaring herself 'unmaternal and apart'; even late in the novel, Esther suspects she would go mad if she 'had to wait on a baby all day' (BJ, 234/222). Proving these fears false, her motherhood acts as a sign that her rehabilitation is complete, and her new life is successful. The society's conformist aspirations for women, as announced by, for example, Adlai Stevenson, are finally accepted and fulfilled by Esther. The bell jar has not descended again—at least, not yet.

However, the destructive social systems remain in place at the end of the novel, and Esther has still not discovered a desirable identity for herself. The reader is given no help in understanding how she has progressed from the hesitant optimism of the concluding pages to her present state as an apparently happy mother some years later. The novel's silence is ambiguous, leaving open the question of how to interpret Esther's recovery: has she overcome the social structures that made her ill, has she been forced to conform to them, or will the bell jar inevitably descend again 'someday' to stifle her? Ted Hughes gives a challenging and optimistic answer:

The main movement of the action is the shift of the heroine, the 'I', from artificial ego to authentic self—through a painful death [. . .] The authentic self emerges into fierce rebellion against everything associated with the old ego. Her decisive act (the 'positive' replay of her 'negative' suicide) takes the form of a sanguinary defloration, carefully stage-managed by the heroine, which liberates her authentic self into independence.[9]

This interpretation follows the novel's mythic scheme of death and glorious rebirth, into which even the name Esther Greenwood clearly fits—Esther is almost a homonym of Easter. But Hughes's distinction between artificial and authentic selves subscribes, rather less tentatively, to the same act of faith as Esther. The evidence for such a positive conclusion is ambiguous; it might equally be argued that far from being 'stage-managed', the 'sanguinary defloration' to which Hughes refers is a potentially fatal haemorrhage after sex, punishing another of Esther's choices. It also seems limiting to argue that sexual freedom, at a literal or symbolic level, is sufficient to solve all the conflicts which lie behind her breakdown. In fact *The Bell Jar* provides no definitive means of judging the success of Esther's treatment. The effect is profoundly unsettling. Giving herself the benefit of hindsight, Esther sounds like an omniscient narrator, until it becomes clear that she remains implicated in the breakdown of her younger self, and is still not free: she reveals a fear in the final pages that her recovery may only have been temporary. Recovery, at the end of the novel, equates to conformity; any reading which identifies unproblematically with Esther's journey must necessarily support her desire to belong to the society which, elsewhere in the novel, she blames for her breakdown.

Like the journal entry where Plath, surrounded by faces, finds herself 'faceless', Esther's search for identity is reflected in her obsessive fascination with faces throughout the novel. This culminates in the last two pages where the word 'face' and its plural appear six times, and where the asylum librarian is described as 'effaced'. Faces, in Esther's descriptions, usually appear disembodied: at Joan's funeral she recognises 'other faces of other girls from college' rather than simply 'other girls from college'; similarly, she sees the town cemetery behind 'the face of the minister and the faces of the mourners' (BJ, 256/242–3). Finally, in the last moments of the novel, as Esther presents herself to the asylum doctors for appraisal, she notices 'the pocked, cadaverous face of Miss Huey, and eyes I thought I had recognized over white masks': 'The eyes and the faces all turned themselves towards me, and guiding myself by them, as by a magical thread, I stepped into the room' (BJ, 258/244). The most curious word in the passage is 'themselves'. Without it, the sentence would still convey the faces' disembodiment, but the addition of 'themselves' heightens the effect, so that the 'eyes and the faces' act independently of the people they belong to. This enhances Esther's sense of danger: at the moment of potential release, she remains isolated, vulnerable and exposed, and must look for 'guidance' to the body language of those around her. At the same time, Esther's perception of identity continues to be fragmented; eyes and faces turn to her rather than people. Despite Ted Hughes's claims for the emergence of an authentic, independent self, at the end of the novel she is still an outsider, unable to engage fully with the whole human beings who constitute her society.

**Notes**
7. Rose, J., *The Haunting of Sylvia Plath* (Virago, 1991), pp. 145–6.
8. See *Revising Life: Sylvia Plath's Ariel Poems*, pp. 122–3.
9. Hughes, T., 'Sylvia Plath: *The Bell Jar* and *Ariel*', p. 5.

MARILYN BOYER ON LANGUAGE AND DISABILITY

Although it could be conjectured that the patriarchal system poisoned Esther, this notion is individuated in the person of Buddy Willard, her boyfriend from Yale. Buddy is staying at a sanatorium to cure his tuberculosis. Buddy's disabled state, though, is different from what will subsequently occur to Esther. Where male disabilities center around questions of "agency" female disabilities are often associated with a "system of shame" (Miner 285). When Esther visits Buddy in the mountains, they attempt to ski on Mt. Pisgah. She is doing fine until a man steps into her path causing her to break her leg in two places. As she falls, her "teeth crunched a gravelly mouthful" and "ice water seeped down" her throat (98). This oral explanation of the effects of the accident indicates substances going down instead of coming out, in a process of silencing and freezing her, while disabling her mouth and her abilities. This happens because a man crossed her path. Nevertheless, this momentary condition does not dissuade her; she wants to ski again until a smiling Buddy informs her that her leg is broken. As she is coming to, looking at Buddy, she sees behind him, "black dots swarmed on a plane of whiteness" (98). Although these dots are people emerging out of a hazy consciousness, it is important to notice how her first reactions are about black and white, that is, the printed word. She sees people as writings, as punctuation marks on paper, visible voices.

Because Esther is temporarily broken, her body is used here as a metaphor for a crippled language which is "in a cast for months" (98). Although people will write upon her, she is, for the time being, halted from fluidity and mobility. Her words become frozen and her vision myopic. Even if one could say that a crippled leg does not hamper one's writing ability, it nonetheless stigmatizes her as "other" in addition to slowing her down because she will need crutches. Her disabled body represents her fractured "corpus" of writing, because she is no longer the doer of actions. Instead, things are done to her: people are "unfastening," "collecting," "pull[ing]" "closing," and "probing" (98). As Esther attempts to ski again, she is "gathering the fragments of a divided, repressed body" and trying to "render noisy and audible all that had been silenced in phallocentric discourse" (Minh-ha 259). In Lacanian terms, then, "as was the case with Freud, it is not in words that the lesson can be learned, but in the body, in one's life" (Felman 20).

It is also most interesting to note how chapter eight ends and how chapter nine begins. There is a definite gap of silence in between the two, which accounts for Plath's/Esther's reaction of silence to her memory of Buddy's telling her that she will be in a cast for two months. The gap also represents the indeterminate number of months that have gone by. It is a stark reaction in any case to leave the reader to continue with the brutal lines of Hilda, another contest winner: "I'm so glad they're going to die" with reference to the conviction of the Rosenbergs who allegedly stole bomb drawings and gave them to the Russians (99). Because this statement comes directly after chapter eight, it could also refer back to Esther's thought-dreams about Buddy's smug contentment that she too would be handicapped for a while after the ski accident. Buddy's outright revenge against Esther is his attempt to escape a feminized perception of himself as passive. This action, resulting in Esther's broken leg, initializes Buddy as an "autonomous male agent" (Miner 188). Situated between the two violent statements, the gap suggests that it should be viewed as a disabled body itself, disjointed, cut off from language, with only space in which to recover, space to remember, or space to settle. For Toril Moi, this body gap is understandably representative, from a phallocentric point of view, of a "necessary frontier between man and chaos" ... where women occupy the unenvied position of marginality, "neither inside nor outside, neither known nor unknown" (213). Irigary would agree that because women cannot fully participate in male discourse without using male language, femininity speaks best "in the gaps, blanks and silences of the text" (Moi 218).

If Buddy Willard had manipulated Esther into skiing down a slope too slippery for her own minimal expertise, another man is equally responsible for her loss of self-esteem because he is not only spiteful, but abusive. At the behest of Doreen, Esther agrees to go on a blind date with Marco, a Peruvian. In order to pave his way with Esther, Marco gives her his diamond stickpin, an object she might have used to later defend herself. But the diamond stickpin is a signifier for marriage rights. In the symbolic gesture of giving Esther the pin, Marco now assumes that there is an understanding between them: she owes him—he will make her pay in some way for being the recipient of the diamond. He intends to "perform some small service worthy of a diamond" (105). In other words, Marco will be reimbursed through his actions for the worth of the diamond.

As he begins to manhandle her by grabbing her arms, Esther labels him as a "womanhater" (106). She states that she believes she was dealt to him as any other card in a deck of "identical cards" (106). The idea of a woman as a card emblematizes the female body as a picture, with marks on it, undifferentiated in value if picked at random among an endless series of duplicates. In this way, Esther reads herself through Marco's eyes as a dispensable element of the pack. But as they dance, Esther who is "maneuvered," is asked by Marco to pretend that she is "drowning" (107). This request extends the anonymity of the playing card metaphor in an increased depersonalization for Esther. Marco's intention is that she totally submit to his will as if she were a dead body, with no cognizance of self-worth or identity of her own.

As Esther follows Marco's lead, she becomes "riveted to him," and the two become like one person on the floor, not through a union, but rather through engulfment (107). The one being is Marco, as Esther becomes absorbed into him. This is not a marriage rite, but a captivity. Marco proceeds to take Esther out to a deserted golf course and assault her both physically and verbally, ripping her dress with his teeth, and calling her a "slut" (109). As Esther punches him in the nose, he pulls out a white handkerchief and "Blackness, like ink, spread over the pale cloth" (109). This blood that Marco sheds and writes indelibly upon a white background, is his text written upon an assaulted, nearly raped, woman in a qualified state of temporary injury. The anxious and terrified Esther, "weary of fruitless attempts to identify with something on the outside, finds the impossible within" (Kristeva 5). She has been thrown into the mud and pinned down: in this disabled state, she creates her story in blood because language eludes her. Instead, she begins to "writhe and bite" as one might do in a turbulent moment (109).

As Marco not only stigmatizes Esther but all women as "sluts," one wonders if he includes within that term his first cousin who spurned his love because she is going to become a nun. Or perhaps the cousin recognizes the sort of man that he is and a nunnery seems a viable alternative. Also, his anger at her refusal might be taken out on all other women as he lumps them into one perception: violated by their own wishes. As Marco demands his diamond back, he deliberately stains Esther's two cheeks with the blood from his nose (110). She is now "marked" and does not wash off the blood. In order not to disturb the blood on her face, her language is impaired because she only speaks through her teeth without moving her lips. Marco, like Buddy Willard, needs to act in order to compensate for his feminized state. His wounded pride and bloody nose are more than he can bear. As his attempt to rape Esther is disrupted, he turns a "horror story to heroic story," by branding her with his primitive life fluid (Miner 287).

Previously, when Esther is on the ground, beneath Marco, she does not speak, but instead, will "writhe and bite" (109). When she is back at the hotel, she refuses to speak in an effort to appropriate her own experience and also to announce her participation in a ritual gone awry. It could be postulated that here the "ritual serves to renew contact with the abject element [i.e., blood] and then to subsequently exclude it" at some future cleansing (Greed 8). She wants to be noticed as one who has paid the price of sexual sisterhood—except that she is still a virgin. The two tattoo lines on her face are a written message for any reader: tribal victory which transcends "cultural mythologies about the body" (Wendell 274). These lines make visible her emotional and tumultuous encounter in which she is "marked" by Marco, and as a scar representing her place within the patriarchal construct of the word "slut," which she did nothing to encourage even if it is her dream to be initiated into the world of sex. The writing on her face is a metaphor for her experience, and her refusal to speak coherently in order not to disturb the configuration on her face represents her desire to communicate in a more concrete, visual way. Even though Marco's blood on Esther's face is a metaphor representing latent atavistic "success," for Esther, it signifies his failure "to set right what was done wrong or incompletely"

(Miner 288). His blood does not signify *her* wound; he is also a disabled party; she, even though psychologically and physically assaulted, is the perpetrator of an attack upon the "traditional gender system" (Miner 286). . . .

In insisting upon the permanence of a bloody tattoo on her own body, a seemingly punished Esther receives, on her way home, the revelation that she will not be allowed to write on paper because she "didn't make that writing course" (114). She falls into a "gap" created by the withdrawal of this "safe bridge over the dull gulf of the summer" (114). In addition to this bad news, she also learns that Buddy Willard is in love with someone else. These two stunning rejections cause Esther to plunge into a deep depression. Her first reaction, though, is a positive one. She decides to write a novel (119). It is through this sequence of events that Esther's mental disability becomes obvious. When she realizes that she has no experiences to write about her mother tells her to learn shorthand, as if without tales to tell the hand is in some way shortened, or withered. As Esther now begins to fall apart at the prospect of taking shorthand for a living, she gets a headache and visually "the white chalk curlicues blurred into senselessness" (122). As Esther retreats from reality, her reading of *Finnegans Wake* becomes distorted. Words become twisted "like faces in a funhouse mirror" while "The letters grew barbs and rams' horns" (122). Language becomes "untranslatable" as letters in a hallucinatory episode, "jiggle up and down in a silly way" (124). Words and letters not only become incomprehensible, but hostile, like Lacan's words that can "undergo symbolic liaisons and accomplish imaginary acts" (Lacan 87).

When Esther visits Teresa, the family doctor, she tells her that she is unable to sleep or read. As she tries to enunciate her predicament, "the zombie rose up in [her] throat and choked [her] off" (126). It is here that her mental depression and her physical or bodily functioning feed upon one another. As she gets to the point where she cannot operate on her own behalf, Esther seeks psychiatric help from Dr. Gordon. When he asks her what is wrong she responds that she cannot read, eat, or sleep, which are all indicators of depression. But she does not mention the state of her writing, in which, as she attempts a letter to Doreen, "the lines sloped down the page from left to right almost diagonally, as if they were loops of string lying on the paper, and someone had come along and blown them askew" (130).

The major depression that Esther experiences throws her body into a disabled state that affects all aspects of her being, especially her thought processes. Her thinking becomes fragmented and her writing is disjointed. Because "thought is as much a product of the eye, the finger, or the foot as it is of the brain," Esther's language does not operate on any physical or mental level (Minh-ha 261). This whole depressive experience that runs through *The Bell Jar* has its roots in Plath's real life. In *Letters Home*, she reflects in an unsent letter to "E" dated 12-28-53, after not getting into Frank O'Connor's writing class at Harvard, the following: "I was sterile, empty, unlived, unwise and unread. And the more I tried to remedy the situation, the more I became unable to comprehend one word of our fair old language" (130).

This severe depression will eventually lead to Esther's shock treatments, which debilitate her even further since they are administered in a barbaric fashion, akin to electrocution. The shocked body is an even deeper representation of the minimalization of language in Esther Greenwood.

In anticipation of the shock treatment at Walton, Dr. Gordon's private hospital, Esther opens her mouth to ask him what it would be like, but "no words came out" (142). She is unable to verbalize her apprehension even before her body is short-circuited. Not one word is uttered by Esther before her botched shock episode. Even as she tries to smile, she cannot because her "skin had gone stiff, like parchment" (143). Therefore, the preshocked body of Esther Greenwood is already emptied of words or reactions that can be interpreted or understood. Barnard suggests that "By the time she becomes Dr. Gordon's patient, her confusion is far advanced; virtually incapable of action, she has become the helpless object of the acts of others. The clumsily applied shock treatment represents the epitome of such acts" (27). The piece of stiff paper, or parchment, which she feels that her body resembles, has yet to be written upon. She is mute, blank, and rigid, like a silent corpse which, exemplifying "the most sickening of wastes, is a border that has encroached upon everything" (Kristeva 3). The writing upon her will be the electric current that will erase her ability to focus or to remember. . . .

After electroshock at Walton, Esther sinks deeper and deeper into a psychotic state. After trying to drown and hang herself, she goes into the basement and overdoses on sleeping pills. Later, after being found, she wakes up in the hospital, unable to see. Wagner-Martin states that "the contortions of sight (she cannot see at all for awhile), hearing, language and the physical appearance (particularly as she gains weight because of the insulin shock treatments) continue Esther's anxiety: nothing is recognized" (78).

Therefore, lying in the hospital bed after her suicide attempt leaves Esther physically scarred, at least temporarily, for as she finally gains back her sight she looks into a mirror and sees that her "face was purple, and bulged out in a shapeless way, shading to green along the edges, and then to a sallow yellow" (174). This face is a "supernatural conglomeration of bright colors" (174). In turn, she smashes the mirror into pieces, creating a kaleidoscopic, more obscure image of herself. She cannot come to terms with "the movements assumed in the image and the reflected environment" (Lacan 1).

The hospitalized, brightly colored, overdosed, failed suicidal body of Esther Greenwood acts as a metaphor for a distorted language in that she experiences herself floating "between the sheets" (171). She is not the writing on paper, but the undercurrent that runs among the pages of a text. Her whole perception of herself is as something off the page rather than on it. Overdosed, she has lost the contiguity with the text of her own body. She is out of her environment, in an altered, inappropriate gap, the underground chamber. She can be located within the nuances of language, the meaning beneath the words, the things unspoken, difficult to comprehend, sometimes violent. The body that she inhabits is the result of violence imposed upon herself through her act of attempted suicide. Between the sheets of Plath's own texts (some of which have been lost or destroyed), she "runs back and forth across the passage of the body into words. In so doing, she identifies within writing a violence which belongs inside the body" (Rose 33). For the person who has undergone such violence, even at her own hand, she describes the suicidal self in the poem "Lady Lazarus":

For the eyeing of my scars, there is a charge

For the hearing of my heart—

It really goes.

And there is a charge, a very large charge

For a word or a touch

Or a bit of blood (58–63).

Extending this perception of the body as brutalized, stigmatized object, for which Plath did use her own personal experiences, it can be argued that "the final question for Esther in her prison-house of language—misnamed, misaddressed, misheard, and misidentified—is, what does language mean? What does language do?" (Wagner-Martin 78). These questions about the meaning and function of language, especially in relation to the body, are constantly at the core of Plath's writing and are never fully answered. There certainly is a "physicality of language" because "language is embodied [. . .] through words" (Rose 33). What language "means" and "does" is an ongoing and ever changing process which Plath plays with throughout her works and her life. It is one of her major themes incorporated in the concept of the "body." Kristeva also delineated the mind/body connection "by insisting both that bodily drives are discharged in representation and that the logic of signification is already operating in the material body" (Oliver, "Kristeva" 1).

136

After Esther's suicide attempt, she decides to make her own language by freeing herself from the symbolic order, and, essentially, it is her "feminist task to prevent patriarchs from silencing opposition" (Moi 221). She uses her body for her own expected pleasure by entering into the world of sexual relations. Even this turns out to be a temporary eruption of limits in which male and female reactions are rendered through ink and blood. With diaphragm in hand, tool of liberation, Esther has her first sexual encounter in Cambridge with a math professor by the name of Irwin whom she meets on the steps of Widener Library, so close to language. This sex act with Irwin hurts her and she bleeds profusely. An indifferent Irwin states "Sometimes it hurts" (229). Even though Esther is concerned about the blood she is shedding, she feels "part of a great tradition" (229). One wonders if this is the tradition of initiation into sex or of sexual abuse. She relates this feeling of belonging to "the stories of blood-stained bridal sheets and capsules of red ink bestowed on already deflowered brides" (229). Looking back at the girls in Dinesen's "The Blank Page," red capsules were probably unknown to them or there would have been no blankness. Esther, nevertheless, applies towel upon towel to soak up the blood from the wound she has received. In this way, where Irwin "initiates action" as the male patriarch will, she, the female, "reacts, adjusts," to her newly found sexual freedom (Miner 289).

The hemorrhaged body of Esther Greenwood acts as the container for blood–red ink which pours out of her, and coincidentally Plath, in volumes. In her poem "Kindness" Plath writes that "The blood jet is poetry, / There is no stopping it" (18–19). What she emits from her womb is her creative force, her "opus," her "valuable" (Plath "Lady Lazarus" 67–68). This sort of writing that she speaks of as a birth process "takes on different qualities in women's contexts" (Minh-ha 259). Blood stains which were once used as a "testimony to the women's function as a silent token of exchange" are, for Plath, representative of the artist who is "bleeding into print" (Gubar 296; 301). Creativity involves "painful wounding" (296). For Kristeva, "the body's inside [. . .] shows up in order to compensate for the collapse of the border between inside and outside" (53). This language that Esther produces onto the towel is the purpose of her whole being; its distortion lies in the idea that blood is usually red, but this blood is so red, it is black, like ink. What one might expect is instead, "one in a million" (233). As she touches the blood, her fingertips also become black. This bodily metaphor is justified by Minh-ha who asserts that "thought is as much a product of the eye, the finger, or the foot as it is of the brain" (261).

Therefore, Esther's encounter with Irwin produces a body of writing. Now she even has something painful to write about: her wound. Writing can be libidinized as in the Derridian fable of "a sexual union in which the pen writes its in/dis/semination in the always folded/never single space of the hymen" (Minh-ha 260). For Esther, all of the production occurs within herself but is organically imprinted like markings on shroud, on a towel, a blank page, a white absorber of hurtful feelings.

## Works Cited

Alvarez, A. *The Savage God: A Study of Suicide*. New York: Random, 1972.

Axelrod, Stephen Gould. *Sylvia Plath: The Wound and the Cure of Words*. Baltimore: Johns Hopkins UP, 1990.

Barnard, Carole King. *Sylvia Plath*. Boston: Twayne, 1978.

Bloom, Harold, ed. *Sylvia Plath*. New York: Chelsea, 1989.

Coleman, Lerita M. "Stigma: An Enigma Demystified." Davis 216–31.

Creed, Barbara. *The Monstrous Feminine: Film, Feminism, Psychoanalysis*. London: Routledge, 1993.

Davis, Lennard J., ed. *The Disability Studies Reader*. New York: Routledge, 1997.

Dinesen, Isak. "The Blank Page." *Last Tales*. New York: Random, 1975. 99–105.

Felman, Shoshana. *Jacques Lacan and the Adventure of Insight: Psychoanalysis in Contemporary Culture*. Cambridge: Harvard UP, 1987.

Goffman, Erving. "Selections from *Stigma*." Davis 203–15.

Gubar, Susan. "'The Blank Page' and the Issues of Female Creativity." Showalter 292–313.

Kristeva, Julia. Trans. Leon S. Roudiez. *Powers of Horror: An Essay on Abjection*. New York: Columbia UP, 1982.

Lacan, Jacques. Trans. Alan Sheridan. *Ecrits: A Selection*. New York: W. W. Norton, 1977.

Lane, Gary, ed. *Sylvia Plath: New Views on the Poetry*. Baltimore: Johns Hopkins UP, 1979.

Malcolm, Janet. *The Silent Woman: Sylvia Plath and Ted Hughes*. New York: Knopf, 1994.

Mazzaro, Jerome. "Sylvia Plath and the Cycles of History." Lane 218–40.

Miner, Madonne. "Making Up the Stories as We Go Along: Men, Women, and Narratives of Disability." *The Body and Physical Difference: Discourses of Disability*. Ann Arbor: U of Michigan P, 1997. 283–95.

Min-ha, Trinh T. "'Write the Body' and 'The Body in Theory'." Price and Shildrick 258–66.

Moi, Toril. "Feminist Literary Criticism." *Modern Literary Theory: A Comparative Introduction*. Ann Jefferson and David Robey, Ed. Totowa: Barnes, 1982. 204–21.

Oliver, Kelly. "Kristeva and Feminism." 29 October 2001. <http.www.cddc.vt.edu/feminism/Kristeva.html>

———. *Reading Kristeva: Unraveling the Double-Bind*. Bloomington: Indiana UP, 1993.

Plath, Sylvia. "Admonition." *Letters Home* 110.

———. *The Bell Jar*. 1971. New York: Harper Perennial, 1996.

———. *The Collected Poems*. Ed. Ted Hughes. New York: Harper, 1981.

———. "The Fifteen-Dollar Eagle." 1959. *Johnny Panic* 91–104.

———. *Johnny Panic and the Bible of Dreams: Short Stories, Prose, and Diary Excerpts*. New York: Colophon-Harper, 1980.

———. *The Journals of Sylvia Plath*. Ed. Karen V. Kukil. London: Faber, 2000.

———. "Kindness." *The Collected Poems* 269–70.

———. "Lady Lazarus." *The Collected Poems* 244–246.

———. *Letters Home: Correspondence 1950–1963*. Ed. Aurelia Schober Plath. New York: Harper, 1992.

———. "The Wishing Box." 1956. *Johnny Panic* 204–10.

Price, Janet, and Margrit Shildrick, eds. *Feminist Theory and the Body: A Reader*. New York: Routledge, 1999.

Rose, Jacqueline. *The Haunting of Sylvia Plath*. Cambridge: Harvard UP, 1992.

Sage, Lorna. "Death and Marriage." Wagner 237–43.

Showalter, Elaine, ed. *The New Feminist Criticism: Essays on Women, Literature, and Theory*. New York: Pantheon, 1985.

Stevenson, Anne. *Bitter Fame: A Life of Sylvia Plath*. Boston: Houghton, 1989.

Thomson, Rosemarie Garland. *Extraordinary Bodies: Physical Disability in American Culture and Literature.* New York: Columbia UP, 1997.

Uprety, Sanjeev Kumor. "Disability and Postcoloniality in Salman Rushdie's *Midnight's Children* and Third World Novels." Davis 366–81.

Wagner, Linda W., ed. *Sylvia Plath: The Critical Heritage.* London: Routledge, 1988.

Wagner-Martin, Linda. *The Bell Jar: A Novel of the Fifties.* New York: Twayne, 1992.

Wendell, Susan. "Towards a Feminist Theory of Disability." Davis 260–78.

Zajdel, Melody. "Apprenticed in a Bible of Dreams: Sylvia Plath's Short Stories." Bloom 149–61.

# KATE A. BALDWIN ON THE NOVEL'S SOCIAL AND POLITICAL CONTEXTS

Understanding the context of both the political and the sexual is crucial and deserving of recapitulation. First, in broad strokes, the political. As I have discussed elsewhere, the Cold War is usually presented as a struggle based on two very different types of ideological power: American capitalism cum liberalism versus Soviet communism cum totalitarianism. This vision of hostile rivalry is based in a binary framework that squares American citizenship against its Soviet other, a framework that during the period enabled some U.S. citizens to determine a sense of self based in opposition to this Soviet other. Cold War critics have elaborated the means by which national narratives helped determine the key connotations and responsibilities of civic membership and participation. These theorizations of narrative's role in building a sense of national community, naturalizing the relationship between people and territory, have created ways of analyzing and better understanding the relationships between subjectivity and citizenship during the Cold War period. Understanding the ways in which narrative can help to create social bonds amongst citizens has been key to a rethinking of the Cold War, its U.S. citizenry, and the reach of its logic through various cultural and social strata.[7] To be sure, *The Bell Jar* participates, with an almost gleeful abandon, in the normalizing rituals of national narrativizing. Esther's search for selfhood through the dramatically opposed lives of poetry and motherhood offers us a character who throws herself against the limited options available to her like a furious pinball, aiming for and then bouncing away from discrete targets of female identity. But in spite of this dramatic pull towards the winning ticket of achieved selfhood, the text also resists an easy repetition of the common sense of American Cold War sociality.

Here lies the sexual. The book strains to reassure us that Esther has emerged from *The Bell Jar* and written the novel that remains as the material fact of her recovery. Esther's rebirth by electroconvulsive shock therapy (ECT) is, however, undercut by the multiple gaps the text summons: we are left with the uncanny sense of suspension.[8] Readers are left to wonder about that space between the novel's end and the writing of the narrative from that location of health and recovery. Ambivalence towards the narratives that would assure us of the protagonist's success in a U.S. Cold War idiom—marriage and motherhood—is made evident within the book's opening pages. Esther mentions "the baby" (presumably hers) once in an aside. Like the offhand comment that names it, "the baby" is brought in like a potted plant and then left unattended. The gap between the space of reputed remission at the end of the book and the opening place of the narrative within a dubious maternal fulfillment opens into a chasm. This space is punctuated by moments that suggest a negotiation of historically specific states of emergency.

The text, after all, opens with the 1953 electrocution of the Rosenbergs. It has been suggested that Ethel Rosenberg can be interpreted as a ghost of Esther Greenwood and, moreover, that Esther's ECT, which serves as the source of her proverbial rebirth, can be juxtaposed with Ethel Rosenberg's death by electrocution.[9] Ethel Rosenberg's status as a bad mother—an image the press went to great pains to construct—stays with Esther as a reminder that she must conform to the era's dictates and be a good mother. However, the consequences of bad motherhood in the 1950s are also, as Philip Wylie's cult of "momism" so forcefully articulated, a vulnerability to outside coercion, a susceptibility to Soviet influence, or, perhaps worst of all, becoming a Soviet. As Andrew Ross has pointed out, the fear of the Rosenbergs was based on a perception of their ordinariness, "not because they harbored subversive, or violently revolutionary views (as Popular Fronters, they did not), but because they were so much like an ordinary, patriotic American couple" (20). At the same time, their liminality as Jews was never far from the surface.[10] The cultural logics of anticommunism, racism, and momism come together through a belief in the enemy within. The novel plays with this tentative logic, stringing along not only Ethel Rosenberg as a kind of Esther *doppelgänger*, but also introducing a Russian woman as a shadow reflection, a woman whom Esther temporarily but lustfully desires to be. By the binary logic of the era that the book so well depicts, the Russian woman must be announced because she is that which U.S. women must not be. Even more so than Ethel Rosenberg she is a sustaining enemy within, the other of U.S. Cold War femininity. . . .

The picture of Russian-meets-American in *The Bell Jar* takes up the terms of the Nixon–Khrushchev encounter and shifts them, offering a link that pursues the feminine specter of translation. We are introduced to the unnamed Russian woman through Esther's much-anticipated date with Constantin, a Russian translator who works at the U.N.: "And while Constantin and I sat in one of those hushed plush auditoriums in the U.N., next to a stern muscular Russian girl with no makeup who was a simultaneous translator like Constantin, I thought how strange it had never occurred to me before that I was only purely happy until I was nine years old" (75). Given all the "hot" issues debated in the summer of 1953—the Korean truce, fears of communism in the Middle East, U.S. trade embargos, the lingering instability following Stalin's death—it is telling that Esther's mind runs from her surroundings to her own troubled sense of self. She stares not at but "through the Russian girl in her double-breasted gray suit, rattling off idiom after idiom in her own unknowable tongue . . . and I wished with all my heart that I could crawl into her and spend the rest of my life barking out one idiom after another" (75). The picture Esther draws for us of the Russian girl conforms to stereotype. "Muscular" and "stern," she defies American femininity, rebuking makeup and wearing a dull, outré double breasted suit.[18] Life magazine may have announced just a year earlier that "Iron Curtain Look is Here!" (rpt. in Filreis ed.), but they were careful to delineate the difference between that "look" and the American one. (You can tell the American girl by her "slender gams.")[19] Yet frumpy as this female is, Esther, the pseudo-fashionista, is still drawn to her, and, more importantly, to her "unknowable" language. The desire to become the Russian girl is not simply about a "negative identity politics" (Davidson 184). Rather, it is about the alarming lure of a particular kind of speech, speech as empty speech. The language of idioms is after all one in which meaning is non-coincidental with the literal. The text thus suggests the simultaneous enticement of national narratives that seem to offer identity as a solution and the foundation of that lure in rhetoric that is overblown, idiomatic, and empty. As Esther comments, to embody the Russian by "crawling inside her" would instantiate a particular kind of removed selfhood, rather than a revelation of the "enemy within," a return to the American-conceived Russian womb of empty speech: the "corner of America in the heart of Moscow."

It is Cold War speech that's empty, and that necessitates articulation and then translation into imprecise idioms. This summoning of female failed cross-cultural exchange does not invoke translation as failure *per se* but rather reflects a desire to feel that emptiness or nothing as *something*, to make non-coincidence a mode of being. It is a criticism of "simultaneous translation" as adequate to instantiate complete knowledge. We could see this as restaging the Nixon–Khrushchev encounter by emphasizing its weird performativity, its slippery, discontinuous production of meaning. As Gayatri Spivak has noted, translation requires a certain intimacy, and in Plath's scene infidelity is exposed as key to the exchange of knowledge about the other. What Esther voices is equal parts enforced misrecognition and desire. We should not forget that Esther's wish to sleep with a Russian, let alone to be a Russian, is alarmingly un-American (taking the parallel to Ethel Rosenberg much further). *The Bell Jar* offers us the opportunity to see U.S. Cold War femininity as caught up in the weird performance—as perpetuated by the U.S. media—of the Soviet other.[20] Indeed, Esther's whole encounter with the Russian woman talks back to a nostalgia for substance and sexual presence in which Esther, as a product of nation-building narratives, seems trapped. And *The Bell Jar* shows us how her desires are constructed through a narrative in which failure presents itself as the most promising alternative. . . .

Similarly, Esther's encounter with a black kitchen worker at Belsize recalls her parallel encounter with the Russian woman. Again, the presence of the kitchen here is not incidental. It underscores the purported absence of race from the Kitchen Debate and likewise from the dilemma of U.S. female captivity during the Cold War. This kitchen worker is introduced as follows: "Usually it was a shrunken old white man that brought our food, but today it was a Negro" (180). The logic of equivalences presented here suggests that the black man is not simply a substitute for a white man, but rather a substitute for a "shrunken old white man." (The worker's masculinity is equivalent to that of a decrepit white geriatric.) If this were not insult enough, he is accompanied by a woman "in blue stiletto heels" who was "telling him what to do."[24] The heels correlate to the insinuated sexuality of white femininity here. The woman's sexuality is lodged in her unavailability to the Negro, and articulates itself as superiority and bossiness: she instructs him, and he obeys while "grinning and chuckling in a silly way" (180). Not only is the black male explicitly emasculated and nameless, thus establishing the sexual economy of taboo that is ingrained in white supremacy, but he also performs his duties with token compliance.

In spite of his namelessness, however, the Negro is the one character in the novel who reads Esther accurately. He listens to her impertinent order "we're not done . . . you can just wait" and responds by calling her "Miss Mucky-Muck," (181). Esther, as no one has yet dared to announce, is a little shit.

She complains when he serves two kinds of beans at a meal: "beans and carrots, or beans and peas, maybe; but never beans and beans," she growls. In retaliation, Esther kicks him and declares, "That's what *you* get" (181–82).[25] Esther's sense of entitlement propels her "you" (as opposed to "I" or "we")— hurling difference in its wake. What the text tells us is that Esther's character is grounded in her relationship to choice. This is her whole problem in a nutshell: she wants it all, but purportedly can't have it. She is the American girl spoiled by choice. However, the text makes explicit here the parameters of that choice, and who is implicated. Her reaction to the kitchen worker is all about his insufficient presentation of choice: the beans and carrots, beans and peas, but never beans and beans. The choice he presents is no choice: it's beans and beans. Faced with this apparent lack of choice, she behaves badly, an indulged brat, as he says, "Miss Mucky-Muck."

The book thus elaborates upon the differential possibilities of choice as they make themselves available to white women and African Americans during this era. Sandwiched between her exchanges with the kitchen worker is a brief scene in which Esther overturns a tray of thermometers so that the mercury balls glisten with potential dispersal, as she says "into a million little replicas," but if pushed together "would fuse, without a crack, into one whole again" (183). The book is clear about Esther's choice in the Cold War asylum: either you chose a million selves or one whole self. But the book also articulates this as a false dichotomy between the fractured and the whole. During this era, the state's demand for a relationship between woman and nation can be extrapolated from a 1950 U.S. National Security Directive that sought to move the subject "in the direction [the state desires] for reasons which [s]he believes to be [her] own" (qtd. in Saunders 4). This anticipation of Althusserian interpellation, in which the state conditions the subject to be an ideal participant, was part of what was termed "psychological warfare" necessary to systematically defeat the Soviets. As Frances Stonor Saunders has noted, such warfare was defined by the government as "the planned use by a nation of propaganda and activities other than combat which communicate ideas and information intended to influence the opinions, attitudes, emotions and behavior . . . in ways that will support the achievement of national aims" (4). Within this context, then, *The Bell Jar*'s emphasis on the cohesion of identity alongside the text's performance of the impossibility of such an identity invites us to query the ways that isolated attention to selfhood and its inadequate fulfillment are correlated through Cold War others so as to produce "emotions and behavior" that will "support the achievement of national aims."

The fiction of integrated selfhood that the asylum offers her is one in which such integration relies on the marginalization, the repeated replication of Negro selfhood as always already broken. This brings us back to Nixon's proclamation of diversity as equal to the abundance of choices. *The Bell Jar* points out that to be a million of herself or one integrated whole is after all not a choice—like the beans and beans it offers no choice. This is the novel's response to Nixon's claims, the binary either/or logic of an era in which to be better or integrated is just another version of being plural—a million self-replicating pieces. What would be diverse would be to open selfhood to difference. In these glances, *The Bell Jar* does just that. Esther notes, "Soon after they had locked the door, I could see the Negro's face, a molasses colored moon, risen at the window grating, but I pretended not to notice" (183). This image presents us with the black worker peering into Esther's prison, but also suggests that he could as easily be peering out from his. What we learn from this passage is that her imprisonment relies in part on his and vice versa. This is, of course, the point that Esther pretends not to notice.

If she and he are each trapped, and his lack of choice is hers, these are not analogous locations. After all, Esther has the fiction of integrated selfhood at her fingertips, whereas he remains with more limited access to that fiction. (She is more at leisure to be herself precisely because she is not one of the others identified by the novel.[26]) The kick tells us that this is no simple parallel, but one that relies on her misrecognition,

146

a misrecognition which is so startling as to produce a kick. But we must recall that it is also the readers who are targets of that proverbial kick in the almost-groin: the "you" is "us." That's what "we" get for buying the logic of *The Bell Jar*, the asylum, the false premise of choice.

So, we might ask, is it only Esther's life that the book holds in balance? If, as Ruth Feldstein has argued, the liberal state emerged during the Cold War as a provenance of racial tolerance that went hand in hand with gender conservatism, *The Bell Jar* parts from such coupling and documents how gender conservatism not only manacled white women but also correspondingly genders black men. Moreover, if Friedan's "feminine mystique" derives in part from a lack of sufficient language to describe the constraints of patriarchy, then *The Bell Jar* responds by documenting how a language was indeed present although perhaps not the one Friedan's book imagined. It was one that linked the discontent of white middle-class women to racial emancipation and the demystification of the Soviet other. The text summons these two key myths to offer rebuttals both to Cold War master narratives and to liberal feminist attempts to counter those narratives (e.g. Friedan).[27] Linked by their status as unnamed but key to the maintenance of Cold War ideology, the Russian woman and the Negro are not coincidental extras—they are the forces that threaten to disrupt Cold War sociality, the circuits of sentiment that continue to plague *The Bell Jar*.

## Notes

7. See my elaboration of this relationship in "Between Mother and History: Jean Stafford, Marguerite Oswald, and U.S. Cold War Women's Citizenship."

8. At the end of the novel Esther emerges as if by marionette strings—"guiding myself by them, as by a magical thread," she recalls in entering the interrogation room, the image with which the novel concludes (244).

9. See Ashe.

10. Ross notes that even if their Jewishness was articulated in "politically secular and Americanized terms," Jewishness in the era was "still massively identified in the public mind with unpatriotic behavior" (20–21).

18. For common stereotyping of the Soviet woman see also "S-x in the Soviet Union:" "Sex with a capital S could very easily distract citizens from the 'building of communism'" (45), and "Allure, Milady? Try Spirit of Red Moscow."

19. Apparently Plath's own "gams" were featured in a student newspaper in Cambridge when she was studying there on a Fulbright in 1955.

20. Esther next removes herself even further from acting on these partial desires: "Then Constantin and the Russian girl interpreter and the whole bunch of black and white and yellow men arguing down there behind their labeled microphones seemed to move off at a distance. I saw their mouths go up and down without a sound, as if they were sitting on the deck of a departing ship, stranding me in the middle of a huge silence" (75). The self-imposed cocoon of isolation is of course not unlike the "white cocoon" of isolation Esther experiences at Belsize, the asylum where she inaugurates a recovery of sorts. In this scene, Esther is of the world but cut off from it: the world is a transnational one of representative "black and white and yellow men," a departing ship of political engagement. Esther is left in silence and it's unclear if she prefers this world-at-a-distance pose, or if the text derides her naïve solipsism which sees "freedom" as escape from the body trapped in its Cold War contradiction. (Esther turns in the next line to recite the "literal" things she can't do, like cook, sew, clean, etc., those mainstays of Cold War femininity.) One critic makes the argument that because Plath underlined the sentence in her copy of Cleanth Brooks's *The Well Wrought Urn*, "The lovers, in rejecting life actually win to the most intense life," writing was "'the enduring immanence' she sought to create," and that through writing, she would be ushered into a better life, a "most intense" one (Hammer 77–78). Yet I wonder if we shouldn't read this causal link between Plath's college-age doodlings and *The Bell Jar* otherwise. Surely being removed from the world, engulfed in a "huge silence" is portrayed in an ambiguous light in which a mockery of the urge to disengage from the world, to be caught in that bubble of silence and navel-gazing apathy, is equally apparent.

24. Qtd. in Saunders 4.

25. Esther moves to a place where no one can see her actions below the waist. She doesn't kick him in the groin—that would be too obvious. Rather she goes for the calf. The orderly gets her point, rolling his eyes at her, or playing the role of accommodating the white woman's antics.

26. These others are referenced through numerous racial and ethnic images throughout the novel and include the "big, smudgy-eyed Chinese woman staring idiotically into my face," (Esther's own reflection in the elevator after her food poisoning); Dodo

Conway, Esther's fecund Catholic neighbor; Mrs. Tomolillo, the Italian American woman Esther witnesses giving birth and then again (falsely) identifies in the asylum; the dark-skinned Dr. "Pancreas"; and Marco, the Peruvian who assaults Esther.

27. "Today American women are awakening to the fact that they have been sold into virtual slavery by a lie invented and marketed by men. One book has named that lie and told women what to do about it," claims the back cover copy of Friedan's *Feminine Mystique*.

## Works Cited

Alarcón, Norma, Caren Kaplan and Minoo Moallem. "Introduction: Between Woman and Nation." *Between Woman and Nation: Nationalisms, Transnational Feminisms and the State*. Durham: Duke UP, 1999. 1–16.

Ames, Lois. "Sylvia Plath: A Biographical Note." *The Bell Jar*. New York: Harper-Collins, 1999.

Ashe, Marie. "*The Bell Jar* and the Ghost of Ethel Rosenberg." *Secret Agents: The Rosenberg Case, McCarthyism and Fifties America*. Ed. Marjorie Garber and Rebecca L. Walkowitz. New York: Routledge, 1995.

Baldwin, Kate A. *Beyond the Color Line and the Iron Curtain: Reading Encounters between Black and Red, 1922–63*. Durham: Duke UP, 2002.

———. "Between Mother and History: Jean Stafford, Marguerite Oswald, and U.S. Cold War Women's Citizenship." *differences* 13:3 (2002): 83–120.

Balibar, Etienne. "The Nation Form: History and Ideology," *Race, Nation, Class: Ambiguous Identities*. London: Verso, 1991.

Baranskaya, Natalya. *Nedelia kak Ndelia* (*A Week Like Any Other*) *Novyi Mir* (11, 1969: 23–55).

"Better to See Once." *Time* August 3, 1959: 11–19.

Borstelmann, Thomas. *The Cold War and the Color Line*. Cambridge: Harvard UP, 2002.

Boym, Svetlana. *Common Places: Mythologies of Everyday Life in Russia*. Cambridge: Harvard UP, 1994.

Brain, Tracy. *The Other Sylvia Plath*. Harlow: Longman, 2001.

Buckley, Mary. "The Woman Question in the Contemporary Soviet Union." *Promissory Notes: Women in the Transition to Socialism*. Eds. Sonia Kruks, Rayna Rapp, and Marilyn B. Young. New York: Monthly Review Press. 1989. 251–81.

Clements, Barbara Evans, Barbara Alpern Engel, Christine D. Worobec, eds. *Russia's Women: Accommodation, Resistance, Transformation*. Berkeley: U of California P, 1991.

Davidson, Michael. *Guys Like Us: Citing Masculinity in Cold War Poetics*. Chicago: U of Chicago P, 2004.

De Hart, Jane Sherron. "Containment at Home: Gender, Sexuality, and National Identity in Cold War America." *Rethinking Cold War Culture*. Ed. Peter J. Kuznick and James Gilbert. Washington: Smithsonian Institution P, 2001.

Epstein, Mikhail. *After the Future: The Paradoxes of Postmodernism and Contemporary Russian Culture*, Trans. and Ed. A. Miller-Pogacar. Amherst: U Mass P, 1995.

Feldstein, Ruth. *Motherhood in Black and White: Race and Sex in American Liberalism, 1930–1965*. Ithaca, NY: Cornell UP, 2000.

Friedan, Betty. *The Feminine Mystique*. 1963. New York: Dell, 1983.

Hammer, Langdon. "Plath's Lives." *Representations* 75 (Summer 2001): 61–88.

Hixson, Walter L. *Parting the Curtain: Propaganda, Culture and the Cold War, 1945–1961*. New York: St. Martin's, 1996.

"Iron Curtain Look is Here!" *Life* (1952). *The Literature & Culture of the American* 1950s. 2 August 2004. Ed Al Filreis. U of Pennsylvania. <http://www.writing.upenn.edu/~afilreis/50s/iron-curtain.html>

"Ivan Takes a Look at American Life: Photo Report from Moscow." *U.S. News and World Report* 10 August 1959: 40–50.

Kaplan, Amy. "Manifest Domesticity." *The Futures of American Studies*. Ed. Robyn Wiegman and Donald Pease. Durham: Duke UP, 2002.

Kennan, George. "The Sources of Soviet Conduct." *Foreign Affairs* 25 (July 1947): 566–82.

Khrushchev, Nikita. *The Great Mission of Literature and Art*. Moscow: Progress Publishers, 1964.

Lehmann-Haupt, Christopher. "An American Edition—At Last," *New York Times* 16 April 1971: 35.

*Literaturnaia Gazeta* 28 July 1959: 2.

Marling, Karal Ann. *As Seen On TV: The Visual Culture of Everyday Life in the 1950s*. Cambridge: Harvard UP, 1994.

May, Elaine Tyler. *Homeward Bound: American Families in the Cold War Era* (Revised) New York: Basic Books, 1999.

Middlebrook, Diane. *Her Husband: Hughes and Plath—A Marriage*. New York: Viking, 2003.

"Nasha replika soroka Amerikanskim redaktoram." *Krokodil* 22:1564 (10 August 1959): 4–5.

Nelson, Deborah. *Pursuing Privacy in Cold War America*. Chicago: U of Chicago P, 2002.

Pease, Donald. "National Narratives, Postnational Narration." *Modern Fiction Studies* 43.1 (1997) 1–23.

Peel, Robin. "Sylvia Plath: Writing, History, and Politics," *Writing Back: Sylvia Plath and Cold War Politics*. Madison, N.J.: Fairleigh Dickinson UP, 2002.

Plath, Sylvia. *The Bell Jar*. 1963. New York: Harper-Collins, 1999.

Plummer, Brenda Gayle. *Rising Wind: Black Americans and U.S. Foreign Affairs, 1935–1960*. Chapel Hill: U of North Carolina P, 1996.

Reid, Susan E. "Cold War in the Kitchen: Gender and the De-Stalinization of Consumer Taste in the Soviet Union Under Khrushchev." *Slavic Review* 61:2 (Summer 2002): 211–52.

———. "Women in the Home." *Women in the Khrushchev Era*. Ed. Melanie Ilic, Susan Reid and Lynne Attwood. London: Palgrave, 2004: 149–76.

Ross, Andrew. *No Respect: Intellectuals and Popular Culture*. New York: Routledge, 1989.

Salisbury, Harrison. "Allure, Milady? Try Spirit of Red Moscow." *New York Times* 3 March 1954: 1–2.

Sandeen, Eric J. *Picturing an Exhibition: The Family of Man and 1950s America*. Albuquerque U of New Mexico P, 1995.

Saunders, Frances Stonor. *Who Paid the Piper? The CIA and the Cultural Cold War*. London: Granta, 1999.

"Special International Report: Encounter." *Newsweek* 3 August 1959: 16.

Spivak, Gayatri. *Death of a Discipline*. New York: Columbia UP, 2003.

Steinbeck, John. *A Russian Journal: with Pictures by Robert Capa*. New York: Viking, 1948.

"The Two Worlds: A Day-Long Debate." *New York Times* 25 July 1959: 1–3.

Whitney, Thomas P. "S-x in the Soviet Union." *New York Times* 1 January 1956: 43–44.

Wylie, Philip. *Generation of Vipers*. 1942. New York: Rinehart, 1955.

Von Eschen, Penny. *Race Against Empire: Black Americans and Anticolonialism, 1937–1957*. Chapel Hill: U of North Carolina P, 1997.

———. *Satchmo Blows Up the World: Jazz Ambassadors Play the Cold War*. Cambridge: Harvard UP, 2004.

## JANET BADIA ON POP CULTURE APPROPRIATIONS OF *THE BELL JAR*

Perhaps because it is Plath's only published novel, *The Bell Jar* has assumed iconic significance in literary and popular culture.[1] One might even say that *The Bell Jar* enjoys its own celebrity, having made cameo appearances in American films as different as *10 Things I Hate About You* (1999) and *Natural Born Killers* (1994). In the first, the novel appears in the hands of the film's central character, Kat Stratford, a cynical, depressed and angry teenage feminist who, in one early scene, defends Plath's status within the literary canon against what she calls 'the oppressive, patriarchal values that dictate our education'.[2] In the latter, the novel can be glimpsed lying face down on the bed next to a sleeping Mallory (née Wilson) Knox just moments before she and her boyfriend Mickey murder her abusive parents and subsequently set off on their cross-country murder spree.[3] References to the novel—and to Plath more generally—are common in television as well, especially those shows that centre on young adult women, such as *Freaks and Geeks* and *The Gilmore Girls*. Nor are such cameos limited to Hollywood. The novels *Sleepwalking* by Meg Wolitzer and *Seven Moves* by Carol Anshaw both depict female characters who, as part of important plot developments within the stories, read *The Bell Jar*. Indeed, there is a certain variety of entertainment in which one just expects to encounter a young woman reading or referencing *The Bell Jar*. One would hardly be surprised to find *The Bell Jar* in the hands of Clare Fisher from the current HBO drama *Six Feet Under* or any of the central characters who plot female revenge in the film *The Smokers* (2000), to name just a couple of examples.

The image has become so common, in fact, that it has even been parodied in an episode of the American cartoon *The Family Guy*. The episode, entitled 'Fish Out of Water' (2002), centres on two parallel plots: Peter, the father of the Griffin family, loses his job, buys a boat and decides to become a fisherman; meanwhile, Meg, Peter's teenage daughter and, according to her, 'the only one in school without plans to go on spring break', sulks about the house, arms crossed in disgust, until her mother, Lois, drags her along for a week at a spa. One early scene in particular sets the stage for an episode about teen angst and ostracism and, of course, a cameo appearance by *The Bell Jar*. In the scene Peter approaches his wife and daughter as they are about to leave on their trip and tells them he will see them in a few days, to which Meg responds, 'Not if I strangle myself with seaweed wraps and die.' Commenting on the obvious, Peter replies in kind: 'Oh, you are dark.' Needless to say, mud baths do nothing to ameliorate Meg's image of herself and the pair leave the spa earlier than planned so that Meg, as she puts it, can 'go home and spend the next three days in solitary confinement where I belong'. On their way home, however, Lois spots a sign for a 'Spring Break Blowout' and, while Meg sleeps, detours to the beach to surprise her pouty teenager daughter. Once at the blowout, it is Lois who enjoys the parties while Meg, disgruntled as ever, struggles to fit in. After one particularly gruelling night of rejection, Meg returns to her hotel room and finds solace in (what else?) *The Bell Jar*.[4]

Because images like this might suggest that Plath, as a writer, need not be taken seriously, most Plath scholars would probably prefer to ignore the fact that Plath and *The Bell Jar* have become fodder for cartoons. Yet the image of the novel in *The Family Guy* should not be overlooked, for it can provide us with an interesting opportunity not simply to consider the fact of the novel's iconic status, but also to think about why the novel has assumed the meaning it has in literary and popular culture. While one's first inclination may be to take the image of Meg reading *The Bell Jar* at face value—that is, as a depiction meant to signal a melodramatic, though no less recognizable, teenage pathology—it is important to remember how much of *The Family Guy* is satire and rather sophisticated satire at that. When placed in this larger context, the image of Meg reading *The Bell Jar* becomes something more than the straightforward depiction of the young adult angst and depression one sees in films like *10 Things I Hate About You* and *Natural Born Killers*.

Consider, for instance, that here we have a cartoon character who is miserable simply because she has been excluded from typical spring-break festivities and who later, when given the chance to participate in the festivities, apparently finds more pleasure sitting in her hotel room reading a novel Plath had once titled 'Diary of a Suicide'.[5] In other words, Meg might be a mopey teenage girl but her gloominess is hardly commensurate with Esther Greenwood's descent into deep depression. Because of this gulf in expectation, one cannot help but wonder just what the show's creators are spoofing with this image of Meg Griffin as a Plath reader. Is the object of the parody the young adult angst that presumably draws Meg to *The Bell Jar*, or is the object of the parody something more original, like the very idea that *The Bell Jar* can function metonymically as a symbol of young women's depression? That is to say, perhaps *The Family Guy* uses the comical image of Meg reading *The Bell Jar* to pose a serious question about whether it is fair to diagnose a young woman's mental state from the book she chooses to read.

However one interprets the image of Meg reading *The Bell Jar*, it does make one point clear: the question of who reads *The Bell Jar* and why they read it has been the focus of much attention within literary and popular culture throughout the novel's history. One could further argue that images of *The Bell Jar*, insofar as they are tied to the question of who reads Plath's writing and why, have been central to determining everything from the novel's literary and cultural value, to Plath's status within the literary canon, to acceptable modes of reading the story the novel tells. Indeed, thinking about the novel's cameo roles in such pop culture arenas as film and television can provide a helpful starting point for examining not only *The Bell Jar*'s association with young adult female angst but also its layered themes and the various lenses that critics have used to interpret those themes since the novel's earliest reception. . . .

Certainly, for many young adult readers—especially women—the appeal of the novel now lies in its reputation. That is to say, reading *The Bell Jar* has become a teenage rite of passage, one frequently initiated by other adolescents and, increasingly today, by mothers and teachers eager to share the novel that had been influential in their own adolescences. But while the novel's reputation might explain why some new readers pick up the novel in the first place, it does not explain the appeal of what those readers find within its pages. If one does seriously entertain the question of this appeal, some interesting avenues emerge.

For example, the apparent desire among critics to control how the novel is read is especially interesting when one considers Esther's own preoccupation with control and self-determination. From her relationship with Buddy Willard and her mother, to her experimentation with suicide methods, to her fight to escape the bell jar, nearly all the plot episodes within the novel reveal Esther's struggles to gain control over her own life, to determine her own choices, rather than merely to accept those that society presents to her. In fact, one could argue that it is Esther's desire and search for control that threads together the many identities Esther struggles with, including her identity as a young woman, a patient, a daughter, a successful student, an aspiring writer and, of course, a potential wife and mother.

In the very first scene of the novel, Plath introduces readers to the general loss of control that Esther experiences as a young woman new to New York City and the publishing world of women's fashion magazines. The narrative of the 1950s middle-class American dream tells Esther that, having won a scholarship to Smith College and now a guest editorship at a fashion magazine, she is supposed to be 'the envy of . . . other college girls just like [her] all over America' (*BJ*, p. 2). The girl in this narrative, Esther explains, is supposed to end up 'steering New York like her own private car'. This kind of control is not, however, what Esther experiences during her stay in the city. As she puts it, 'I wasn't steering anything, not even myself. I just bumped from my hotel to work and to parties and from parties to my hotel and back to work like a numb trolley-bus' (*BJ*, pp. 2–3). Later, when faced with the options of going to a fur show with Betsy and the other guest editors, going to Coney Island with Doreen, or staying in bed by herself, Esther experiences a similar paralysis: 'I wondered why I couldn't go the whole way doing what I should any more. This made me sad and tired. Then I wondered why I couldn't go the whole way doing what I shouldn't . . . this made me even sadder and more tired' (*BJ*, p. 30).

Underlying Esther's feeling of paralysis is her inability—or, if one prefers, her rebellious refusal—to make choices about her life. Unlike many women of the 1950s who did not have access to the relative social mobility Esther enjoys, she does have many life choices before her; a result, in part at least, of her success as a student, which, as she herself acknowledges, has prepared her to take any number of career paths. In one of the central metaphors of the novel, Esther imagines these choices in her life as a green fig tree branching out before her, with one fig representing 'a husband and a happy home and children', another fig representing 'Europe', others representing an academic career, publishing, poetry; and 'beyond and above these figs were many more figs [she] couldn't quite make out' (*BJ*, p. 77).

Because Esther's fear of her own inadequacy constantly overwhelms her, she cannot see the fig tree and the choices each branch represents in a positive light. She is simply crippled by such choices: 'I saw myself sitting in the crotch of this fig tree, starving to death', she says, 'just because I couldn't make up my mind which of the figs I would choose ... choosing one meant losing the rest and, as I sat there, unable to decide, the figs began to wrinkle and go black' (*BJ*, p. 77). Reminding us of the way her last name, Greenwood, reflects the fig tree, Esther's damaged self-image turns the once-green branches into rotten, dreadful choices that fall, spoilt, to her feet.

While many readers today might wish to find themselves faced with so many promising options, Esther's frustration is not unreasonable given the societal constrictions regarding women's roles in mid-century America and what Plath once described as 'The great fault of America', namely, its 'expectancy of conformity' (*J*, p. 411). As her description of the withering figs makes clear, the problem is not that she lacks choices or even that none of the options appeals to her; the problem lies in her desire to have what society tells her is impossible, 'two mutually exclusive things at one and the same time' (*BJ*, p. 94). Just as importantly, Esther is told again and again that her choices, while hers to make, will have repercussions she cannot control. She might opt to be both a mother and a poet, for example, but the state of marriage and motherhood in mid-century America, as Buddy Willard tells Esther, dictates that 'after [she] had children [she] would feel differently, [she] wouldn't want to write poems any more' (*BJ*, p. 85). At best, then, the process of choice for Esther has been circumscribed by societal rules and expectations—rules and expectations that tell her to be one, and only one, thing, despite her own inclinations. At worst, the process of choice is completely denied her.

This is perhaps nowhere more clear than in Esther's struggle with her sexuality and the possibility of pregnancy. In the chronological time of the narrative, one of the first examples of this struggle occurs in her relationship with Buddy. On a visit to his room at Yale, Buddy introduces the topic of sex by asking Esther if she would like to 'see' him naked (*BJ*, p. 68). Esther indulges him, but then dismisses him when he asks her to reciprocate by letting him 'see' her. The thought of standing naked in front of Buddy does not appeal to her at all, but the invitation prompts her unexpectedly to ask Buddy if he has 'ever had an affair with anyone' (*BJ*, p. 69). Because Buddy has presented himself as sexually inexperienced throughout their relationship, Esther expects him to say 'no'. After all, as her mother tells her, Buddy was 'a nice, fine boy . . . the kind of person a girl should stay fine and clean for' (*BJ*, p. 68). But, of course, Buddy has had an affair and when he discloses the extent of his relationship with the waitress, Esther quickly reexamines their sexual interaction. As she explains, 'from the first night Buddy Willard kissed me and said I must go out with a lot of boys, he made me feel I was much more sexy and experienced than he was' (*BJ*, p. 70). Clinging to her pride, Esther is forced to bottle her indignation, an indignation that springs not so much from Buddy's transgression as from her realization that she has never had control over her own sexual identity in her relationship with Buddy. As she explains, it was not the thought of Buddy's previous relationship that concerned her: 'What I couldn't stand was Buddy's pretending I was so sexy and he was so pure, when all the time he'd been having an affair with that tarty waitress and must have felt like laughing in my face' (*BJ*, p. 71). As these passages make clear, not only does Esther discover that she has been made the butt of Buddy's joke, she also realizes that she is subject to societal double standards that understand a young man's sexual experiences as 'sowing wild oats' but then judge a young woman's sexual experiences as 'promiscuity'. In other words, what she realizes is that Buddy can construct his own sexual identity while she cannot.

Dismayed by this sexual double standard (*BJ*, p. 81), Esther attempts to seize control over her sexuality by losing her virginity to someone other than Buddy. But as we know from the scene of sexual assault she has already narrated by this point in the novel, even her virginity—or rather her decision to lose it and to whom—is potentially subject to the control of men like Marco, the Peruvian 'woman-hater' (*BJ*, p. 160) who spits, "'Sluts, all sluts. . . . Yes or no, it is all the same'", after Esther successfully fights off his attempt to rape her (*BJ*, p. 109). Furthermore, Esther can never have complete control over her sexuality because, while the choice to lose her virginity to Irwin is finally her own, the possibility of pregnancy, like the bell jar, always looms over her. This fact is one her mother tries to impress upon Esther by giving her the *Reader's Digest* article 'In Defense of Chastity', which, as Esther characterizes it, attempts to compel young women to choose chastity until married, out of fear of rejection by a future husband and because there is 'no sure way of not getting stuck with a baby' (*BJ*, p. 81). To someone as adamant about not wanting to have children as Esther is at this stage, the possibility of pregnancy makes the decision to lose one's virginity a perilous choice at best. For Esther especially, the risk is 'a baby hanging over her head like a big stick, to keep her in line' (*BJ*, p. 221). It is perhaps no wonder then that Esther, in her determination to gain control by losing her virginity, tries to convince herself that the thought of pregnancy 'hung far and dim in the distance and didn't trouble [her] at all' (*BJ*, p. 80).

It is also important to remember that when Esther does finally sleep with Irwin, she does so only after she has been fitted for a diaphragm, an act that underscores why birth control is such an apt synonym for contraception. Yet even the moment of her fitting for the birth control device ironically reveals the limited control that society actually allows Esther to exercise over her own sexuality. As Esther explains, birth control is illegal in Massachusetts at this time and it is only with Dr Nolan's help that she is able to see a doctor who can fit her for the diaphragm. Nor does she have the money herself to pay for the medical service. She must rely instead on the money that Philomena Guinea has given her as a get-well present, money that would surely have been denied Esther had her benefactress known how it would be spent. But despite the obstacles of access and money, Esther sees birth control as her path to self-determination. In her words, 'Whether she knew it or not, Philomena Guinea was buying my freedom' (*BJ*, p. 221). Perhaps for the first time in the novel, Esther expresses full self-possession: 'I am my own woman', she says to herself as she rides back to the asylum with her purchase (*BJ*, p. 223).

## Plath's prose and the question of value

While it is true that *The Bell Jar* has become the iconic work of Plath's oeuvre, a metonym even of Plath herself, the question of the novel's place within Plath studies remains very much unanswered. On the one hand, the fact that new editions of the novel seem to arrive perennially on bookstore shelves would seem to support the claim that *The Bell Jar*, like *Ariel*, is a major piece of Plath's oeuvre, at least in the minds of general readers whose interest presumably generates the republication of the novel in its various forms, including a 25th Anniversary edition and an Everyman's Library edition. On the other hand, the work still receives less scholarly attention than the poetry. Perhaps the difficulties in deciding the novel's value lie with Plath herself, who, in ways she could not have anticipated, established a framework for the evaluation of her own work. While in a letter to her mother she described the poems that would eventually form the volume *Ariel* as the 'best poems of [her] life'—poems that would 'make [her] name'—she instructed her mother to 'Forget about the novel and tell no one of it. It's a potboiler and just practice' (*LH*, pp. 468, 477). The implication of words like 'potboiler' and 'just practice' suggest, of course, that Plath saw her novel as inferior to her poetry. Yet on another occasion, Plath described her poetry as 'an evasion from the real job of writing prose' (*JP*, p. 3).

These seeming contradictions in Plath's own descriptions of her prose and poetry point to her complex ambitions as a writer, a writer who wished to have the cash rewards that went with successful story writing but whose talents seemed to be better suited to poetry. In the end, perhaps it is this tension between her professional drive and her talents that produces the reluctance among scholars to isolate *The Bell Jar* as an independent work whose value does not depend on its relation to the poetry. Or perhaps the reluctance more complexly reflects the anxieties that generally surround Plath's prose writing. . . .

That so much of our understanding of *The Bell Jar* and Plath's other prose writing has become entangled with anxieties about readers seems both inevitable and ironic. In the end, it might be that the anxieties speak not to the quality of Plath's prose but to a larger desire among critics to protect Plath, who, after all, had no opportunity to reflect on the place of her prose within her entire published oeuvre. Whatever the explanation, the reasons for the anxieties matter less than what the anxieties themselves can teach us about Plath's prose writing, particularly *The Bell Jar*. No matter how much critics might wish to divorce the novel from its popularity among young women especially, there is no getting around *The Bell Jar*'s iconicity. The best we can do as we approach *The Bell Jar* is be mindful of its association with Plath's most devoted readers and the ways it unavoidably seeps into our interpretations of the novel's meanings and value.

## Notes

1. References throughout are to the American editions of *The Bell Jar* (New York: Harper & Row, 1971) and *Johnny Panic and the Bible of Dreams* (New York: Harper & Row, 1979).

2. *10 Things I Hate About You*, directed by Gil Junger (Touchstone Pictures, 1999).

3. *Natural Born Killers*, directed by Oliver Stone (Warner Brothers, 1994).

4. Seth MacFarlene, 'Fish Out of Water', *The Family Guy* (Fox, 2001).

5. Robin Peel, *Writing Back: Sylvia Plath and Cold War Politics* (Madison: Fairleigh Dickinson University Press; London: Associated University Presses, 2002), p. 66.

# Works by Sylvia Plath

(The dates reflect the first American editions of the works.)

*The Colossus and Other Poems*, 1962

*Ariel*, 1966

*Three Women: A Monologue of Three Voices*, 1968

*The Bell Jar*, 1971

*Crossing the Water*, 1971

*Winter Trees*, 1972

*Johnny Panic and the Bible of Dreams*, 1979

*The Collected Poems*, 1981

*The Journals of Sylvia Plath*, 1982

*The Unabridged Journals of Sylvia Plath*, 2000

Annotated Bibliography

Alexander, Paul, ed. *Ariel Ascending: Writings about Sylvia Plath*. New York: Harper & Row, 1985.

A collection of essays on Plath and her works. Includes pieces by Joyce Carol Oates, Elizabeth Hardwick, and Rosellen Brown.

Axelrod, Steven Gould. *Sylvia Plath: The Wound and the Cure of Words*. Baltimore: Johns Hopkins University Press, 1990.

Combining psychoanalytical, feminist, and intertexual methods, Axelrod explores the personal and literary influences on Plath.

Barnard, Caroline King. *Sylvia Plath*. New York: Twayne Publishers, 1978.

In-depth analysis of *The Bell Jar* and Plath's poetry, examining her voice and the nature of her perception.

Bennett, Paula. *My Life a Loaded Gun: Dickinson, Plath, Rich, and Female Creativity*. Chicago: University of Illinois Press, 1990.

Important feminist analysis of *The Bell Jar*. Argues that a woman's true self, asserting itself against patriarchal culture, is necessary for the creation of art.

Bonds, Diane S. "The Separative Self in Sylvia Plath's *The Bell Jar*." *Women's Studies* 18 (1990): 49–64.

Argues that the recovery Plath constructs for Esther only re-enacts the fragmentation of identity and leaves Esther to define herself in relation to culturally ingrained stereotypes of women.

Brain, Tracy. *The Other Sylvia Plath*. London: Longman, 2001.

Instead of focusing on Plath's emotional struggles, focuses on her identity as a writer. Includes close readings of her stories and poems and examines unpublished letters and typescripts of *The Bell Jar*.

Bundtzne, Lynda K. *Plath's Incarnations: Woman and the Creative Process*. Ann Arbor: University of Michigan Press, 1983.

Analyzes *The Bell Jar* as an allegory of femininity and focuses on Esther's development.

Cornell, Elaine. *Sylvia Plath: Killing the Angel in the House.* West Yorkshire: Pennine Pens, 1993.

A brief guide to Plath's biography and her critical history, combined with interpretations of Plath's works, including *The Bell Jar*.

Gill, Jo, ed. *The Cambridge Companion to Sylvia Plath.* Cambridge: Cambridge University Press, 2006.

Collection of essays by leading international scholars that provides a comprehensive overview of the place Plath's poetry, prose, letters and journals occupy in twentieth-century culture.

Kendall, Tim. *Sylvia Plath: A Critical Study.* London: Faber and Faber, 2001.

Examines Plath as a working writer, focusing on her poetry and *The Bell Jar.*

Macpherson, Pat. *Reflecting on The Bell Jar.* London: Routledge, 1991.

Study of Plath's novel in relation to the history of the feminist movement and the evolution of feminist literature; also situates the novel alongside discourses of the 1950s, including cold war politics and normative heterosexuality.

Malcolm, Janet. *The Silent Woman: Sylvia Plath and Ted Hughes.* London: Picador, 1994.

Explores Plath's life, her posthumous existence and influences, and the difficulty biographers have in penetrating her personal history and her husband's role in it.

Middlebrook, Diane. *Her Husband: Hughes and Plath—A Marriage.* New York: Viking, 2003.

Scholarly work that infuses the reading of Hughes and Plath's marriage with an analysis of their poetry and prose. Hughes and

Plath worked to reconstruct themselves for posterity through their writings, often with conflicting self-portraits.

Peel, Robin. *Writing Back: Sylvia Plath and Cold War Politics*. Madison, NJ: Farleigh Dickinson University Press, 2002.

Analyzes the degree to which Plath's writing was influenced by the politics of the early cold war era.

Plath, Sylvia. *Letters Home*. Aurelia Schober Plath, ed. New York: Harper & Row, 1975.

More than six hundred letters written mostly to her mother, from the beginning of Plath's college years in 1950 to her death in 1963.

————. *The Unabridged Journals of Sylvia Plath*. Edited by Karen V. Kukil. New York: Anchor Books, 2000.

First comprehensive volume of Plath's journals and notes from 1950 to 1962. The newly revealed writings portray an even more complex psyche struggling to create in the face of powerful demons.

Rose, Jacqueline. *The Haunting of Sylvia Plath*. Cambridge: Harvard University Press, 1992.

Addresses why Plath is such an icon. Argues that Plath demonstrates the importance of an inner psychic life for the wider sexual and political world.

Wagner, Linda W. *Sylvia Plath: The Critical Heritage*. New York: Routledge, 1988.

Collection of early reviews of Plath's work.

Wagner-Martin, Linda W. *The Bell Jar: A Novel of the Fifties*. New York: Twayne/Macmillan, 1992.

Looks at the novel in the context of the larger social and historical forces shaping women's lives in America during the 1950s and 1960s. Focuses on issues of gender, genre, and narrative voice.

# Contributors

**Harold Bloom** is Sterling Professor of the Humanities at Yale University. He is the author of 30 books, including *Shelley's Mythmaking*, *The Visionary Company*, *Blake's Apocalypse*, *Yeats*, *A Map of Misreading*, *Kabbalah and Criticism*, *Agon: Toward a Theory of Revisionism*, *The American Religion*, *The Western Canon*, and *Omens of Millennium: The Gnosis of Angels, Dreams, and Resurrection*. *The Anxiety of Influence* sets forth Professor Bloom's provocative theory of the literary relationships between the great writers and their predecessors. His most recent books include *Shakespeare: The Invention of the Human*, a 1998 National Book Award finalist, *How to Read and Why*, *Genius: A Mosaic of One Hundred Exemplary Creative Minds*, *Hamlet: Poem Unlimited*, *Where Shall Wisdom Be Found?*, and *Jesus and Yahweh: The Names Divine*. In 1999, Professor Bloom received the prestigious American Academy of Arts and Letters Gold Medal for Criticism. He has also received the International Prize of Catalonia, the Alfonso Reyes Prize of Mexico, and the Hans Christian Andersen Bicentennial Prize of Denmark.

**Howard Moss** was a poet, critic, dramatist, and poetry editor of the *New Yorker* magazine for more than three decades, until his death in 1987. He received the National Book Award for poetry for his *Selected Poems* in 1971.

**Vance Bourjaily** is a noted author of novels, magazine articles, and stage and television plays. He has been a journalist, co-founder and editor of the journal *Discovery* (1951), and a faculty member at Oregon State University and the University of Iowa's Writers Workshop.

**Robert Scholes** is professor emeritus of modern culture and media at Brown University. An American literary critic and theorist, he is known for his ideas on fabulation and metafiction.

**Linda W. Wagner** is the editor of *Critical Essays on Sylvia Plath* and *Sylvia Path: The Critical Heritage*.

**E. Miller Budick** is the author of *Emily Dickinson and the Life of Language: A Study in Symbolic Poetics* and has published essays on a number of nineteenth- and twentieth-century American writers.

**Diane S. Bonds** is the author of "The Separative Self in Sylvia Plath's *The Bell Jar*" and has served as the assistant to the dean of the Candler School of Theology at Emory University.

**Paula Bennett** is professor of English at Southern Illinois University. She is the author of *My Life a Loaded Gun: Female Creativity and Feminist Poetics* and editor of *Nineteenth-Century American Woman Poets: An Anthology*.

**Pat Macpherson** is the author of *Reflecting on The Bell Jar* and *Reflecting on Jane Eyre*.

**Tim Kendall**, a professor at the University of Exeter, is an English poet, editor, and critic. His latest book of poems, *Strange Land*, appeared in 2005. He has published critical studies on Paul Muldoon, Sylvia Plath, and, most recently, English war poetry.

**Marilyn Boyer** received her Ph.D. in English language and literatures from Fordham University. She is the author of "The Treatment of the Wound in Stephen Crane's *The Red Badge of Courage*."

**Kate A. Baldwin** is associate professor of American studies at Northwestern University. She is the author of *Beyond the Color Line and the Iron Curtain: Reading Encounters between Black and Red, 1922–63* (2002).

**Janet Badia** is an associate professor in the English department at Marshall University. She co-edited *Reading Women: Literary*

*Figures and Cultural Icons from the Victorian Age to the Present* (2005), with Jennifer Phegley. She has published several essays on Sylvia Plath.

Acknowledgments

Howard Moss, "Sylvia Plath, Dying: An Introduction." From *Whatever Is Moving*, pp. 176–181. Boston: Little, Brown and Company. Copyright © 1981 by Howard Moss.

Vance Bourjaily, "Victoria Lucas and Elly Higginbottom." From *Ariel Ascending: Writings about Sylvia Plath*, edited by Paul Alexander, pp. 135–138. New York: Harper and Row. Copyright © 1985 by Paul Alexander.

Robert Scholes, "Esther Came Back Like a Retreaded Tire." Copyright © 1971, *The New York Times*. Reprinted by permission.

Linda W. Wagner, "Plath's *The Bell Jar* as Female *Bildungsroman*." From *Women's Studies*, vol. 12, 1986, pp. 55–64, 67–68. Copyright © 1986 Gordon and Breach Science Publishers, Inc. Reprinted by permission of Taylor and Francis, http://www.informaworld.com

E. Miller Budick, "The Feminist Discourse of Sylvia Plath's *The Bell Jar*." From *College English*, vol. 49, no. 8, December 1987, pp. 875–880, 882–885. Copyright 1987 by the National Council of Teachers of English. Reprinted and used with permission.

Diane S. Bonds, "The Separative Self in Sylvia Plath's *The Bell Jar*." From *Women's Studies*, vol. 18, 1990, pp. 53–61, 63–64. Copyright © 1980 Gordon and Breach Science Publishers, S.A. Reprinted by permission of Taylor and Francis, http://www.informaworld.com

Paula Bennett, "Bonds of Women." From *My Life a Loaded Gun: Dickinson, Plath, Rich, and Female Creativity*, pp. 124–131, 280. Copyright © 1986 by Paula Bennett. Reprinted by permission of Beacon Press, Boston.

Pat Macpherson, "The Motherly Breath of the Suburbs." From *Reflecting on The Bell Jar*, pp. 41–44, 46–51, 53–55, 56. Copyright © 1991 Pat Macpherson. Reproduced by permission of Taylor & Francis Books UK.

Tim Kendall, "Conceiving a Face: Plath's Identities." From *Sylvia Plath: A Critical Study*, pp. 52–59, 221. London: Faber and Faber Limited. Copyright © 2001 by Tim Kendall.

Marilyn Boyer, "The Disabled Female Body as a Metaphor for Language in Sylvia Plath's *The Bell Jar*." From *Women's Studies*, vol. 33, 2004, pp. 206–210, 213–215, 217–220, 222–223. Copyright © 2004. Reprinted by permission of Taylor and Francis, http://www.informaworld.com

Kate A. Baldwin, "The Radical Imaginary of *The Bell Jar*." From *Novel: A Forum on Fiction*, vol. 38, no. 1, Fall 2004, pp. 24–26, 30–32, 34–36, 37–40. Copyright Novel Corp. © 2004. Reprinted with permission.

Janet Badia, "*The Bell Jar* and Other Prose." From *The Cambridge Companion to Sylvia Plath*, edited by Jo Gill. Copyright © 2006 Cambridge University Press. Reprinted with the permission of Cambridge University Press.

Every effort has been made to contact the owners of copyrighted material and secure copyright permission. Articles appearing in this volume generally appear much as they did in their original publication with few or no editorial changes. In some cases, foreign language text has been removed from the original essay. Those interested in locating the original source will find the information cited above.

# Index

## A

achievements, 32, 39, 121
adolescence, 72, 74
adolescent readers, 13, 154
African Americans, 144–147
alienation, 21, 37, 69
alternate identities, 63–66
ambition, 33
Anshaw, Carol, 152
*Ariel* (Plath), 10, 13, 159
authentic self, 102, 128
authority, 70
autobiographical elements, 12, 18, 59

## B

baby imagery, 7, 30, 62, 64, 78, 141
Badia, Janet, 18–19, 33, 151
Baldwin, Kate, 48, 53, 140
baptism, 24–25
Barnard, Caroline King, 36, 43
bathing, 24–25
bell jar image, 49, 50, 57, 58, 61, 66–67, 76, 113–114, 119, 125
*Bell Jar, The* (Plath)
    autobiographical elements, 12, 18, 59
    critics views of, 14
    as female coming-of-age novel, 18, 69–79
    feminist discourse in, 80–91
    pop culture appropriations of, 151–160
    publication of, 10, 12–13
    reception of, 13
    social and gender conventions in, 112–121
    social and political contexts of, 140–147
    summary of, 18–58
Belsize, 50, 52, 56

Bennett, Paula, 19, 26, 54, 99, 103
Berryman, John, 10
Betsy (character), 16, 22–23, 25, 28, 63
Beuscher, Ruth, 12
bildungsroman, 18, 69–79
biography, of Plath, 9–11
birth control, 76, 100, 110, 158–159
blood imagery, 38, 55, 64, 98, 131–133, 137–138
Bloom, Harold, 7–8
Bonds, Diane S., 33, 46, 58, 92
Bourjaily, Vance, 63
Boyer, Marilyn, 23–24, 128
Brontë, Charlotte, 7–8
Brown, Rosellen, 97
Browning, Elizabeth Barrett, 117
Buckley, Jerome, 69
Buddy Willard (character), 22, 40, 57, 115–117, 118–119, 124
    illness of, 35–36, 128–129
    overview of, 15
    relationship with, 29–31, 35–36, 64, 73, 74, 76, 157–158
    skiing incident and, 36, 129–130
Budick, E. Miller, 80
Bundtzen, Lynda, 110

## C

Cal (character), 44–45
camouflage, 60
Caplan, 50
characters, 15–17
childbirth, 30, 39, 73, 76, 79, 99, 119–120
children, 39
city, 70
clothes, 38, 105
cold war, 20, 67, 114, 140–147
*Collected Poems, The* (Plath), 10

*Colossus, The* (Plath), 10, 12
comfort, 26
coming-of-age novel, 18, 69–79
confessional poets, 10
conformity, 25
Constantin (character), 16, 32, 34, 63–64, 101, 124, 142
contraception, 54–55, 76, 100, 110, 158–159
Coyle, Susan, 93
critical reception, 14
*Crossing the Water* (Plath), 10
cultural pressures, 19
cynicism, 23

**D**

"Daddy" (Plath), 10
death, 44, 45, 81
  of father, 46
  imagery, 22
  preoccupation with, 20
Dee Dee (character), 97–98
defamiliarization, 67–68
depression, 39, 41, 133–134
detachment, 44–45
diaphragm, 76, 100, 110, 111, 158–159
disability, 128–131
disclosure, 60
disconnection, 23–24, 37, 44–45, 48, 59–60
disembodiment, 24, 127–128
disgust, 7, 63, 68, 124
distortion, 61
Doctor Gordon (character), 16, 41–44, 65–66, 87, 109, 119–121, 133–134
Doctor Nolan (character), 49–54, 75–76
  basis for, 12
  Joan's suicide and, 57
  overview of, 16–17
  relationship with, 87, 95, 97, 100, 102, 104, 109–110

sexual freedom and, 110–111, 123–124
Dodo Conway (character), 39, 62, 76
domesticity, 39, 46, 93, 107–108, 115–117, 122
Doreen (character), 16, 22–25, 28, 60, 63, 71, 86–87, 95, 125
double standard, 31, 33, 111, 157–158
drowning, 45

**E**

Ehrenreich, Barbara, 115
electricity, 85–87
electroshock therapy, 20, 42–43, 50, 52–53, 60, 66, 67, 85, 87, 109, 119–120, 134–135, 141
Elly Higginbottom (alter ego), 42, 55, 63, 65, 71, 122
empathy, 49, 60–61
Esther Greenwood (character)
  confusion felt by, 26–27
  disconnectedness of, 23–24, 37, 44–45, 48, 59–60
  erratic behavior of, 38
  father's death and, 46
  hospitalization of, 47–55, 55–59, 66, 135–136
  identification with, 13
  identity crisis of, 18–19, 24, 31–32, 59, 70–71, 72, 103–104
  medical establishment and, 41–44, 65–66
  mental breakdown of, 18, 38–44, 46, 61, 75–76
  narration by, 126
  negative encounters with men by, 37–38, 55, 64, 74–75, 99–100, 124, 130–133
  New York experience of, 20–22, 38, 70, 75, 104–106
  overview of, 15
  passivity of, 37, 75
  perspective of, 19–20, 22, 42

quest for identity by, 121–128
rebirth of, 89–90, 91–102
recovery of, 55–59, 77–78, 97,
    102, 127
relationship with Buddy, 29–31,
    35–36, 40, 57, 64, 73, 74, 76,
    115–119, 157–158
similarities to Plath, 12
suicide attempts, 44–47, 62,
    65–66, 83–84, 135–137
views of marriage, 34–35, 57,
    107–108, 116–118

**F**
faces, disembodied, 24, 48, 127–
128
*Family Guy* (cartoon), 152–154
female psychiatrist, 49–50, 109–
110
female role models, 22–23, 71–72,
    103–111, 122–124
female roles, stereotypical, 18, 94
female sexuality, 82, 144, 157
femininity, 19, 27, 106, 144
feminist discourse, 14, 80–91, 123,
    147
feminist perspective, 18
fig tree image, 32–33, 73–74, 108,
    156
films, 151–152
financial insecurity, 27, 159
*Finnegans Wake* (Joyce), 26, 40, 59,
    62
first-person narration, 19–20, 44,
    126
flashbacks, 70
food, 25–26, 28, 82
food poisoning, 71–72, 94–95, 122
foreshadowing, 30, 40
fragmentation, 19, 22
Frankie (character), 23
Friedan, Betty, 147
future
    blank, 41
    fear of, 40

**G**
gender conventions, 112–121
gender roles, stereotypical, 18, 33,
    94, 122
Gilbert, Sandra, 105
graphic imagery, 30
guilt, 25, 76

**H**
heart of winter image, 88–90
heterosexuality, 54, 56, 96
Hilda (character), 37
homophobia, 53–54, 56, 98
hope, 50
hospitalization, 47–59, 66, 135–136
hostility, 68
Hughes, Ted, 9–11, 13, 126–127,
    128

**I**
ideal life, 21
identity
    alternate, 63–66
    conflicting, 31–33, 72
    disconnected, 48
    fragmentation of, 19
    heterosexual, 54, 56
    quest for, 70–71, 103–104,
        121–128
    uncertain, 24
identity crisis, 18–19, 24, 31–32,
    59, 70–72, 103–104
illness, 28–29, 60–63, 128–129. *See
    also* mental illness
inadequacy, 32
insecurity, 27, 159
integrated selfhood, 146–147
irony, 59, 72, 75, 78, 100, 137
Irwin (character), 17, 55, 57, 102,
    110

**J**
*Jane Eyre* (Brontë), 7–8
Jay Cee (character), 16, 26, 27,
    71–72, 80–83, 95, 123

Joan Gilling (character), 29, 50–56, 125
  as alter ego, 53, 66, 97, 101
  lesbianism of, 53–54, 75, 95–96, 97–98, 99, 100–101
  overview of, 17
  suicide of, 57–58, 97, 100, 110–111
*Journals of Sylvia Plath, The* (Plath), 11
Joyce, James, 26

**K**

Kendall, Tim, 28, 58, 121
Kitchen Debate, 144
kitchen mat, 34, 93, 116
Kukil, Karen V., 11

**L**

*Ladies' Day*, 105–106
"Lady Lazarus" (Plath), 10, 136
Laing, R.D., 61, 66
language, 81–83, 90, 129, 130, 133–134, 136–138
Lenny Shepherd (character), 23, 23–24
lesbianism, 53–54, 56, 75, 95–101
*Letters Home* (Plath), 10
love, 63
Lowell, Robert, 10
Lucas, Victoria (pseudonym), 10, 12

**M**

MacPherson, Pat, 112
Marco (character), 16, 37–38, 55, 64, 74–75, 124, 130–133, 158
marriage, 18, 29, 30, 32–36, 46, 57, 107–108, 116–118, 156
marriage proposal, 35–36
masculinity, 68, 85–87
medical establishment
  control of women by, 30, 50, 119–121
  distrust of, 41
  failure of, 44, 65–66

patriarchal power of, 18, 19, 41–42, 49–50, 87, 89
  view of mental illness by, 43
medical imagery, 30
men, 33, 54, 70
  attitude toward, 110
  negative encounters with, 37–38, 55, 64, 74–75, 99–100, 124, 130–133, 158
mental breakdown, 38–44, 46, 75–76
mental illness, 18, 19, 43, 46, 60–63
mercury, 48
Moi, Toril, 130
Moss, Howard, 7, 20, 49, 59
motherhood, 18, 34–35, 39, 46, 76, 107–108, 114, 116–118, 126, 141–142, 156
Mrs. Greenwood (character), 15, 33–34, 39, 45–46, 51–52, 56–57, 75, 78–79, 95, 108–109
Mrs. Norris (character), 50
Mrs. Willard (character), 15, 29, 32, 33, 34, 42, 116, 117–118

**N**

narration, first-person, 19–20, 44, 126
narrative
  dual, 84
  national, 141–143
  structure of, 19, 69–79
national narratives, 141–143
*Natural Born Killers* (film), 151, 153
near-death experience, 36
New York City, 20–22, 38, 70, 75, 104–106
Nixon-Khrushchev encounter, 142, 143
Norton, Dick, 118

**O**

O'Connor, Frank, 9, 12, 134

**P**

pain, 30
paranoia, 42, 48
passivity, 37, 75
patriarchy, 18, 41–42, 49–50, 87, 89
period piece, 7
Perloff, Marjorie, 93–94
Philomena Guinea (character), 12, 16, 27, 49, 123, 159
Plath, Aurelia Schober, 9
Plath, Otto Emile, 9
Plath, Sylvia
    biographical sketch of, 9–11
    as legendary figure, 13–14
    prose of, 159–160
Plath, Warren, 9
point of view, 19–20
political context, 140–147
pop culture appropriations, 151–160
power, absence of, 74
pregnancy, fear of, 54, 62, 76, 110, 157, 158
premarital sex, 31, 33, 111, 157–158
Prouty, Olive Higgins, 12
pseudonyms, 63–66
psychiatry, 60, 109–110
Pulitzer Prize, 10
purity, 23, 24, 31, 33–34, 36, 38, 94–95

**R**

rape, 38
realism, 66–68
reality, dissociation from, 24–25, 38, 42
rebirth, 53, 56, 58, 77, 89–90, 92–102, 125, 127
reflections, distorted, 24, 47–48
Rich, Adrienne, 96
roman à clef, 12
Rose, Jacqueline, 123

Rosenbergs, 18, 20–21, 37, 43, 46, 53, 64, 67, 69, 85, 130, 141–142

**S**

Saunders, Frances Stonor, 145–146
Scholes, Robert, 53, 66
self-detachment, 30
*Seven Moves* (Anshaw), 152
Sexton, Anne, 10
sexual aggression, 37–38, 74–75, 130–133
sexual freedom, 54–55, 76, 100, 110, 111, 123–124, 158–159
sexual purity, 31, 33–34
sexuality, 30, 55, 144, 157
Shklovksy, Viktor, 67
shock therapy. *See* electroshock therapy
Showalter, Elaine, 81
sickness, 28–29, 60–63, 128–129
silence, 24, 60, 129–130
*Six Feet Under* (TV series), 152
skiing incident, 36, 129–130
sleeping pills, 41, 46–47
*Sleepwalking* (Wolitzer), 152
*Smokers, The* (film), 152
social context, 140–147
social conventions, 112–121, 126
society
    of 1950s, 18, 28, 33, 70–71, 156–157
    double standard in, 31, 33, 111, 157–158
    expectations on women by, 32–33, 70–71
Spacks, Patricia Meyer, 72
stains, 25
Steiner, Nancy Hunter, 107
Stevenson, Adlai, 107, 126
suburbs, 112–115
suffocation, 40
suicidal thoughts, 44, 45, 61
suicide, 42, 44, 56–58, 62, 97, 110–111

suicide attempts, 12, 44–47, 62, 65–66, 83–84, 135–137
symbols/symbolism
    bathing, 24–25
    bell jar, 49, 50, 57, 58, 61, 66–67, 76, 113–114, 125
    of electroshock therapy, 43
    food, 25–26, 28
    kitchen mat, 34, 93, 116
    New York clothes, 38, 75
    stains, 25
    vomit, 25, 28–29, 60
    womb, 47, 83–84, 89, 90
sympathy, 49, 60–61

**T**

teenage angst, 18
*10 Things I Hate About You* (film), 151–152, 153
tenderness, 100–101
*Three Women: A Monologue of Three Voices* (Plath), 10
tire image, 92–93, 125
trophy mentality, 23–24

**U**

*Unabridged Journals of Sylvia Plath, The* (Plath), 11

**V**

Valerie (character), 50, 58
virginity, 33–34, 54, 55, 63, 68, 158

voice, lack of, 24
vomit, 25, 28–29, 60

**W**

Wagner, Linda W., 23, 37, 42, 55–56, 69, 92–93
wifehood, 116–118. *See also* domesticity; marriage
*Winter Trees* (Plath), 10
Wolitzer, Meg, 152
womanhood
    *Ladies' Day* version of, 105–106
    models for, 22–23, 71–72, 103–111, 122–124
womb, 47, 83–84, 89, 90
women
    in 1950s society, 18, 28, 32–33, 70–71, 156–157
    choices facing, 32–33, 73–74, 76, 107, 145, 146, 155–157
    control of, by medical establishment, 30, 50
    cultural pressures on, 19, 32–33
    stereotypes of, 58, 94, 99, 101, 122
    types of, 22–23, 38
Wymark, 50

AUG 3 2011

DISCARD

RYE FREE READING ROOM
1061 BOSTON POST ROAD
RYE  NEW YORK  10580
(914) 967-0480